# AGAINST ALL ODDS

## A HARLEM STORY

By Walter Wilson

To Johnny Clemmons
a gift from
Colvin Curry

May God encourage you
in your faith as you
read this account of
of another man
saved by grace

RW Walter

Library of Congress Control Number:
2006908495
Publisher: Booksurge, LLC
A Division of Amazon.com

For retail purchases go to Amazon.com

For information regarding special discounts
for bulk purchases go to
www. Booksurge.com
1-866-308-6235
orders@booksurge.com


Manufactured in the United States of
America
ISBN-1-4196-4930-2

AGAINST ALL ODDS, A HARLEM STORY
Is dedicated to the memory of
Lamar Terrell Wilson, my son. He was
killed before his time.


Cover photo taken by:
Mrs. Dorothy Wilson

# TABLE OF CONTENTS

# Acknowledgements

This book would not have begun without the help of Sandy Van Dyk. She was the first to encourage and support me in the creation of this work. Her efforts were followed by Harry Brockington, my brother-in-law who spent countless hours transcribing my recordings. Harry is a poet in his own right.

Much later I was encouraged by my god daughter, Felicia Barnwell, because of her willingness to help in any way she could. Though a teenager, she guided me through the basics of using a computer and Microsoft. Francois Akpovo picked up where Felicia left off. His expertise in the use of computers fine tuned my necessary skills to complete this manuscript. In the final analysis I want to thank God for Raenetta Sylcott. Without her help I would not have produced this work at this time.

## Reviews and Comments

What a candid account of one man's "spiritual rags to riches" story! Rev. Walter gives us an up close and personal experience with poverty, racism, the drug world, jail, and his amazing deliverances. He is intentional, focused and makes things happen. It's a privilege to be called his friend.

Rev. Andrew and Donna Puleo, New York Metro Director, The Navigators

------------------------------------------------------------

Walter Wilson's story is both representative and unique. He speaks for those whom Malcolm X called "the victims of Democracy," particularly black males growing up in an urban context where society's inequities and injustices are exacerbated by the importation of drugs and its resulting criminality. On one level, Walter's story is a criminal narrative—it shows how a bright and promising young man succumbed to the destructive social and spiritual forces that pervaded his world. He writes frankly about the fact of racism and white supremacy—a fact as real in the upper echelons of the drug world as it is in the world of politics and business. Walter's story is disturbing, a no-holds-barred confession of crime and criminality, pride and lust, and brilliance in the service of sin.
But his story is also a conversion epic, a confession that resonates with the same blunt truth of the autobiographies of Malcolm X and Saint Augustine. Walter Wilson is not just a black man struggling at the nadir of the post-Civil Rights era. He is a fallen man in rebellion against God, who will not bend his knee in prayer or acknowledge the claims of righteousness until encountered by the powerful word of God. Like Augustine, Walter is saved by a voice compelling

ii

him to take up the Bible and read. But instead of a shaded garden, the Bible he finds is lying on the floor of a drug den.

The writer's voice is honest and his motivation is earnest. His story chronicles a sojourn from the lowest levels of sin and rebellion to the rising road of grace and freedom in Jesus Christ. "Join me as we take the cause of the Kingdom of God to the next level," Walter Wilson challenges. Read his story and take the challenge.

Rev. Louis A. DeCaro, Jr., Ph.D., author of On the Side of My People: A Religious Life of Malcolm X

-------------------------------------------------------------------

"Against All Odds" is an inspiring story of my father's journey from reproach, to redemption, to restoration. As his daughter, I did not know the Walter Wilson that was reproachable, our relationship fell victim to the streets and the deviant behavior my father worshipped, but I can attest to the relationship that now exists with the Walter Wilson that has been redeemed and now worships God. In today's society where dysfunctional parent-child relationships are a commonality, "Against All Odds" is a testament to restoration, it provides hope and inspiration for every man, woman, and child wounded by circumstance, that God can bring life into any relationship and restore all that life's circumstances have robbed you of, even AGAINST ALL ODDS.

Tesha McMinn

# Foreword

I consider the opportunity to collaborate in the writing of this book as a gift from God. Early December 2004 Reverend Walter Wilson spoke on cult religions and Islam during a series of Wednesday night services. The series was titled "Will the Real God Please Stand up ". He poured out a message that not only educated us, the body of Christ, but also unbelievers on the deceptions and misconceptions behind cult religions. His message also gave us a clear understanding of our fortune in Christ Jesus.

As he presented his message, God gave me this vision. Rev. Wilson began to glow and from his belly a fountain formed. From that fountain water flowed as many came up to drink. The majority of the partakers were young Black men whose thirst was quenched after many years of exposure to false religion and street gangs. As they drank they became healed and delivered on the spot.

I didn't know what to do with this vision. What was God showing me? Then God spoke and said two things,

> "And again, when he bringeth in the first-begotten into the world, he saith, And let all the angels of God worship him. And of

the angels he saith, Who maketh his angels spirits, and his ministers a flame of fire."(Hebrews 1:6-7)

And

"And they overcame him by the blood of the Lamb, and by the word of their testimony; and they loved not their lives unto the death." (Revelations 12:11)

After some prayer and meditation on this word, God revealed to me that Reverend Walter Wilson must write his testimony!

That evening I addressed the issue. I approached Reverend Walter and asked if anyone ever suggested that he write his testimony. He informed me that he already began the process. I shared the vision with him and he thanked me for sharing it. That was all. Was I not hearing God correctly? Reverend Walter already had something written and I was not the first to share this with him. What now, Lord?

Some weeks later I approached him again and he said he might be interested in completing the work but wasn't sure if the Lord was allowing time for him to do it. Once home, I wrote him a letter explaining what the Lord was telling me and volunteered to help him. Weeks later I emailed him writing samples and set up meetings to explain why I was the best person to help in the process, considering I had never written a book. I felt God appointed me to do the job.

After weeks of interviews and life changing events and circumstances, here we are with a book. God has moved in an awesome way. Out of obedience came this, Walter Wilson's testimony. My exposure to and cultivation of this story has helped me to understand some of the issues of the Christian Black man. My prayer is that the readers will make room for God in their lives. He is the only one who will bring hope, joy, love, and freedom like never before. I know my life will never be the same.

My life has been changed by what I have seen and heard since I began this assignment. Rev. Walter's life story proves that God does restore relationships, he pulls you out of trouble, he grants you chance after chance, and most importantly he promises you salvation if you believe in His son.

This is my testimony from this experience, "According to my earnest expectation and my hope, that in nothing I shall be ashamed, but that with all boldness, as always, so now also

Christ shall be magnified in my body, whether it be by life, or by death. For to me to live is Christ, and to die is gain. But if I live in the flesh, this is the fruit of my labour: yet what I shall choose I wot not." Philippians 1:20-22 (King James Version)

Through the spirit of the living God I present you with hope. Enjoy and be freed, filled, and fortified.

Sister Raenetta Sylcott

# The Reason for This Book

Welcome to the life and times of a career criminal. We hear crime/criminal and we feel fear and think violence and vulgarity. Though these elements are encompassed in the criminal arena, they are not exclusive to the underclass. I will attempt to open the reader's eyes to a different perspective. To offer a perspective that encompasses the views of an everyday citizen through his own eyes, unobstructed by rose-tinted glasses. Not clouded by the shadows of the learned and biased. Looking back over my life leaves much to be desired. Personally, all things considered, I believe I've done fairly well, but when I look at the condition of our society, and the conditions facing African Americans especially, my heart aches.

I grew up in an era of change. Social, technological, informational and scientific advances dominated my world. Ideals were espoused and promises made in abundance, only to find we are collectively worse off now than we were in our beginnings. For sure, there have been improvements observed and experienced. We have excelled individually and assumed heights our fore fathers only dreamed about, yet I fear the horror of our forefathers if they could see us now. I can feel their heartfelt grief over their sacrifices having only produced an integrated yet disconnected people. There is so much information bombarding us. We have lost our ability to discern truth, goodness and righteousness. We have descended from the heights of unmerited injustice to the depths of individualism. It's all about me. I have to get mine. Do whatever it takes. We have sacrificed morality on the cross of me-ism and then we complain about the disintegrating world around us.

I too was caught in that tide. Caught up in the era of social transition, but I desire to return to a time and place of sanity. Not go back in time, but perfect our times. I do not declare myself to be anyone special. I am not rich, highly educated, exceptionally gifted or anything else. I am a layman who is not ashamed of who I am or my people. I am in my right mind. I have a decent heart, fair health and I love my people without question. I believe we are challenged with an unprecedented opportunity. I have walked in Christ for over 25 years and I know many who have known him the majority of their lives. Here's the value of this fact. I'm still here. That is the most remarkable thing of all. A black man is still here as we all are. There is untapped value in that fact. I've lived on both sides of life; right and wrong. I've experienced life as a career criminal and as an upstanding member of my community. As a criminal my goal was to get rich or die trying. I thought I knew what I was doing, but I later found out that there was no prize to be had, just death and more sorrow.

On a larger scale I was, unknowingly, a part of a greater conspiracy to eradicate hope in the African American community. This was being accomplished through my participation in crime, immoral behavior, drug use and trafficking. Though I was up to no good and to some, no good to society, I prospered. I grew in stature and prominence amongst my peers. I was hero and villain, friend and foe. I was respected and feared. I disappointed many people and destroyed many relationships. Most of all I broke my mothers heart. From a distance she watched and I am assured she prayed.

In 1979 I believed I knew enough about life and everything in it. I believed all I had accomplished was under my control. That was when I began to feel what I now know was the presence of God and from then on things were different.

Everything that followed led to my salvation. There was complete change in the course of my life. Does God speak in a room filled with drug induced, socially rejected castaways of humanity where God himself is rejected? Yes, He would and He did. Over the next few years I was presented with new opportunities. New relationships were established old relationships were restored. I was further blessed with the honor to get to know my mother as a woman and to see her heart. My community began to accept me as a man of integrity and not as a predator. God gave me a new reputation. He restored my marriage, established my relationships with my children and so much more.

I have come to realize who I am as a participant in the bigger picture of life. I am a survivor. I'm a doer. I am someone who has made a claim on what is available to improve my conditions. I am a self-made man living by my wits. I am a man who is completely sold-out for Jesus. I am a man who believes in hope. I know that the account of my life will impact many who are caught up in the life of drugs, gangs, and guns. Maybe it will affect someone who can't put down the narcotic because there is nothing better to pick up that comforts as thoroughly. Maybe someone's ties to their family and friends have been severed and feel as if reconciliation is impossible. Or maybe you too have prospered and are doing well, but a deep sense of dissatisfaction lingers down in your heart and snatches the joy from your life. Well, there is hope. I pray my story inspires you to hope, to ask, to seek, and to knock on the door of life. I desire with all my heart that a fair chance be given to all who read this book. I desire to encourage you to express the innate ability God has placed within you. I desire for you to survive and for us to overcome.

# Chapter One

Most consider life to begin on their birthday. That is the point an individual enters life on this earth. Our arrival here is a culmination of people and events that cannot be accurately traced to its beginnings. Along with ones comings there are spiritual and other unexplained realities also at work that collaborate with ones ancestry, history and heritage to produce a unique you. In the beginning I didn't know that.

My beginnings erupted from the melding of two family histories. That merging created an individual that continued a trajectory fulfilling the purposes laid out because of decisions I made in life. This story is about coming to life, learning to live and coming of age. Here is my account.

I was born on July 1, 1950 with some drama. My mother said she had a hard time bringing me into this world. She told me I was born unexpectedly. My father was not home when her labor began. She was immediately taken to the old Metropolitan hospital in Manhattan. Before she could reach the hospital I was delivered with the umbilical cord wrapped around my neck. It was touch and go for a few minutes, but my life was saved. That was the beginning of the trouble I would give her in life. My birth at the time was a joyous event nonetheless. Because of that difficulty my birth certificate wasn't officially issued until 1955 (5 years later) in time for me to start school.

My father was born in Savannah, GA in 1926. My mother was born in Camilla, GA in 1928. My maternal grandmother, Weldon, moved her family to Savannah when my mother was still a young girl. It was there my mother met and married my father. My parents migrated from Georgia to New York in 1946 to take advantage of the employment opportunities they were hearing about in the cities up north. They were the first of their respective families to venture to the Big Apple.

Shortly after arriving in New York my parents began their own family. My two older sisters, Rebecca and Betty, were born in 1947 & 1948 respectively. My parents lived at 246 West 131$^{st}$ Street, a walk-up tenement between 7 th and 8$^{th}$ Avenues in Harlem. Because Harlem was under one of its many developmental stages my parents were relocated to 430 East 106$^{th}$ Street after the housing in their area was condemned to allow for the construction of the Saint Nicholas Housing Projects. The government was creating opportunities for those with low incomes to live in newly built housing. Those who would live in them called these developments, the Projects for short.

Two years after my birth my mother with father and three children in tow moved again to set up an awkward existence in the Saint Nicholas Housing Development. It was then my mother, Dorothy Cunningham-Spicer-Wilson, made means for her mother, sisters and brothers to join her in the Big Apple.

The ancestral history of both my parents has been traced back to the early 1800's. I was surprised to find how much information was available. Over the years family reunions have been arranged for both sides of the family. The knowledge possessed by the older members date back to the period earlier referenced. Other information was attained from census tracks and local newspapers. We were fortunate that a segment of the family has remained in the same areas of Georgia for generations.

In the census of 1870 my great, great grandfather Shadwell is mentioned. In 1870 he was 80 years old. He named one of his children Snow. Snow married Mary. It would be interesting if her maiden name could be discovered. From their union five children were sired: Wiley, Johnnie, Shad II, Snow Jr. and Binney.

Wiley Wilson married Alice Jordan. They had nine children. They were William, Jasper, Shad III, Marie, Solomon, Lawrence, Henry, and two other children whose names are not known.

Shad III, my paternal grandfather married Rebecca Taylor September 24, 1919. They had twelve children. The names of their children: Leroy, Rosa Lee, Marrion, Walter, Eloise, Rosa Bell, Millie, Randolph and four other children whose names are unknown. Walter Wilson, my father was the seventh child born from that union.

My maternal ancestral line has been traced back to 1835 to Pelham Georgia in Mitchell County. That was the year my great, great, great grandfather, Rev. Braxton McCoy was born. He died October 10, 1914 at the age of 79. His wife Minerva was born in 1843 and died February 25, 1915 at the age of 72. They were slaves together on the same plantation. It is believed they met and married there. Together they gave birth to fifteen children. Amanda my great, great grandmother was the oldest of their offspring.

Amanda married George Washington of Camilla Georgia in Mitchell County. She gave birth to eight children. My mother vaguely remembered three of them. Corine, the oldest, was my great grandmother. She was born in 1886 and died in 1924 at the age of 38. No additional information was available concerning the cause of her death.

Corine married Dennis Cunningham from Tampa Florida. She gave birth to four children. My grandmother Weldon was the second oldest. My grandmother gave birth to eight children. My mother, Dorothy is the oldest of her children. My grandfather's name was Morris Spicer.

Most of the newly installed inhabitants of the projects were just like us. They were blue-collar working class individuals who migrated from the South who could trace their family histories at least to the 1800's, maybe the 1700's. Many of them, including my mother never lived in a big city, much less New York City and they struggled to adapt to its pace and pulse. My mother kept to herself while living in the projects. Most of the adults did. We children, on the other hand, had more freedom and less fear. We thought the world was ours and we didn't believe anything would stop us. Back then children were safe playing outdoors. We had the run of the projects. There was no gang warfare or drugs in the projects as there were in other areas of Harlem.

During the days of my innocence I had so much fun. It seemed I had it made.

When the projects were constructed the builders started in the center and built outward. 277, 255, 237 and 217, the buildings on the 127th Street side, were completed before the buildings on the 131st Street side. My grandmother and my mother's younger sisters and brothers moved into 277. My sisters, brothers and I played on the 127th Street side of the complex watched over by my younger aunts and uncles.

The projects were full of children. Sharon, Karen, Diane Hicks, Bem-Bem, Baby teeth Harry, Barry, Junio, Zander, Boo, One Leg Poochie, Boo-Boo, Pee Wee, Ernest, Cecil Saulter, Marvin Carter, Donald Jones, the Jeffersons, Jacobis, Bumpers, DeBerrys, Gants and countless more. These are some of the children and families that gave the Saint Nicolas projects its identity and character. Some were more distinctive than others, but all lent their unique presence to the whole mix. I look back and wonder at times what happened to many of them. Few of those early relationships remain. Some persisted longer than others. I am sure that many have already passed on. Sometimes I run into someone from those early years and I am saddened by what I see.

In March of 1954 my bother Keith was born. He was my best friend, and we got into various kinds of trouble together as he grew older. Later I took that giant step to 8$^{th}$ Ave., which drove us down two different paths.

As a male child, I had the liberty of playing without much supervision or rules. At the age of 5 my behavior began to change. I didn't have any interest in school. The teaching methods, tools and styles catered mostly to girls. Here's the routine; we'd enter the classroom, greet the teacher, "Good morning Mrs. Ward ," as we sat at our desks with hands folded. It was monotonous and boring. I didn't care about adults or showing respect in such a way. It wasn't that I was disrespectful. I just didn't have any regard for them. Adults weren't a part of my world. I didn't pay much attention to them.

I was a smart kid. I was able to do the work without trying very hard which left me bored and unattended. You can imagine what would happen. I'd get into some kind of trouble. Eventually I just quit going to school. I began to play hooky as a common practice. I'd find things to do in the street. I'd walk up and down 125th Street and no one thought it strange that a five-year-old boy was alone on 125th Street. I'd go into Woolworth's and steal. That was easy. I'd find kids to play with, food to eat. I'd steal from fruit stands, candy stores, wherever. When it was time to go home, I'd find a hydrant and wash up so that no one knew I was in the streets all day. Somehow my mother always found out and I would get a whipping. The next day she would send me back to school with my sisters. I would wait until they were out of sight and I would sneak away. This was the way it was for some time.

My playing hooky arose from this one incident. While I was still going to school I stole five dollars out of my grandmother's purse. I didn't even know the value of five dollars, but I knew it was money. So, I go to the store and buy some- French fries for my sister and a bag of potato chips for myself. Understand that back in those days French fries were 10 cents and the potato chips cost 5 cents, so I went to school with all this change, $4.85. While in the bathroom, this boy named Philip is there and I'm bragging about all my money. I flash the money and he asks for a dollar. I tell him, no. So, he tells Ms. Ward our teacher. 1955, no Negro five-year-old child is supposed to have that amount of money, so she approaches me about it. "Where did you get the money?" she asks. I wouldn't answer the question so she tells me to bring my parents to school the next day. I was afraid to tell my mother anything. I believed it was safer not to return to school. Eventually my mother found out and took me back to school and the whole affair was brought to light.

In December of 1956 my youngest brother Darryl was born. We used to call him Peachie when he was very young. By then I was in the first grade. I was placed in class 1-207. I was required to attend another session in school with some other students. This was the class for the problem students. Mostly boys were in the class. I guess I had to attend that class because of my behavior in kindergarten.

I had no problems or incidents in first grade. A lot of the children in my class were very disruptive and required a lot of attention from the teacher. I settled down and was able to do the required work satisfactorily. At the end of the school year I placed in class 2-1 for the second grade.

Early in the school year I contracted Ring Worm. My mother cut off all my hair and applied a home remedy as a cure. Boy did it stink. I looked a sight for weeks. The kids at school never let up. I was called blacky, darky, skinny, nasty, baldy and ugly. That was not the only time kids called me names.

In May we had a fashion contest in my class. All the students were asked to dress up. I was so excited. I asked my mother if I could wear the suit I wore on Easter Sunday. She would not let me. Instead she dressed me in a short pants outfit. It wasn't ugly, but I had skinny legs, as my sisters would often remind me. Not only did I not win, the students laughed at me because of my skinny legs. Leroy the boy who won wore his Sunday suit. I never wore short pants again until I was well into my 20's.

My brother, Keith, had grown enough for us to play rough together. We used to wrestle and jump on our bed when our mother wasn't looking. One day while jumping up and down on the bed I fell and bumped my head on the radiator in the apartment. The blood came gushing and I started screaming. My mother rushed me to the hospital after applying first aid at home. By the time we got there I was no longer in pain. The moment the doctor pulled off the bandage my mother prepared the open gash on my forehead began to hurt. What was wrong with my mother and the doctor I thought? I wanted to be left alone. I threw a fierce tantrum kicking and screaming. None of it helped. The doctor probed, cleaned and stitched my forehead. All I knew was that I wasn't in pain when I got there and this man made the pain come back.

In third grade I wanted to get into Mrs. Delgado's class. She was the prettiest teacher in the school. Everybody said she was the best teacher and wanted to be in her class. I didn't make it. I ended up in class 3-2. I didn't want to be in my allotted class. I don't know for sure if I acted out because of that. I do know I was up to my tricks again. I began to steal with a vengeance. Each week the teacher would collect the milk money and the money for the students' savings accounts. Each week I would devise a way to steal it. I was doing this regularly. My teacher began to suspect it was someone in the class so she decided to set a trap.

She did two things. One, she put nail polish on the money she collected and then she put it in the usual place and two, left the room. I told the students we needed to erase the black board. The erasers were kept on the teacher's desk. When several students got up to get the eraser, true to form, I took the money.

When she returned with the principal the money was gone. They lined everyone in the classroom up and I began to get nervous. I thought I'd get caught for sure this time. But I hid part of the money in someone else's pocket in the coat closet and kept the rest of the money for myself. They searched everyone on the line. When they searched me they found some of the marked money. When questioned I denied taking it. I lied and said my mother told me to go to the bakery to buy a loaf of bread from the Taystee Bread factory after school. Of course this made perfect sense to me. Once a week I had to go to the bakery to buy bread after school.

"This is my mother's money; my mother gave me this money to go buy bread from the bakery. Un-un this is not your money!"

I lied, lied and lied. I would never confess. Not in this lifetime. I never told the truth when I would get caught. You don't do that. You go down with your beating. There was no way I was going to tell on myself. I was going down with the lie on my lips. They did find the rest of the money in the coat pocket and that person got blamed, but the principal called my mother in and spoke to her expressing their concern regarding my stealing money from the school. They decided to send me to see a psychologist.

I wonder what they would have done if they had known that I was stealing more than the money from my classroom. After all the students were dismissed I would sneak back into the school and steal anything that captured my attention. My favorite place to go was to the teacher's lockers hoping to find one left open. Sometimes I would get lucky and find someone's purse or wallet left unattended full of money.

I do not know what arrangements my mother made to register me with the psychologist. It was not something I gave any thought to at the time, but one morning before school my mother informed me that I was scheduled to see the psychologist after school. She wrote out all the instructions and made sure I understood where to go and what to do. I was going to have to see the psychologist alone. I was not afraid. I used to travel all over the city alone because Mom taught me how to travel. By the time I was in the third grade I was able to travel as far as 8$^{th}$ Street to get my union glasses. That was more than twenty miles from my home to a world I know I didn't belong in.

When I arrived at this place, the kiddie psychologist office on 123rd Street and Broadway, I felt like this was a waste of time. I thought the doctor was stupid. I mean he asked me stupid questions. He put me in the sandbox to play. He asked me if I liked to play with sand. I wouldn't answer. I just sat there and he would watch. Afterwards he gave me the inkblot test. He'd ask, "What do you see?"

I'd say, "A butterfly."

I'd answer that way over and over. Every picture looked like a butterfly. I hated being there. I felt trapped. Those visits were something that I had to do to get out of trouble. I had no interest in helping them in their observations but I wanted to get out of there as fast as I could. I couldn't understand what was going on. I had a problem facing the world but I also had a problem with the fact that no one explained what was going on. I was thrown into this environment and expected to deal with it. That was inconsiderate, but I didn't blame my mother, she didn't know either.

I had a bitterness that said you couldn't do this to me. So, I decided not to see the psychologist anymore. I know I only went once or twice. But after that...Ha, I was done with that psychologist! Each week I pretended to go to the doctor's office and each week I would come home and give my mother a fictitious account of what took place at the doctor's office. Until finally I told my mom I didn't have to go any more.

There was a benefit I derived out of that situation; I learned a lot about 125th Street and Broadway. I had not ventured that far west before. I had new stomping grounds.

In the fourth grade I was a nervous wreck. I believe it was due to problems at home between my mother and father. There was a lot of discontent on my parent's part. I was viciously biting my nails. I chewed on them so badly I developed an infection on my left thumb. My mother used a burned hatpin to pierce the painful swelling. A nasty yellowish green slime oozed from my thumb. It really did hurt. I don't know if it was my mother's intent, but her treatment of my thumb broke me from the habit of biting my nails.

Each year every class was assigned a science project. The projects were to be completed by the spring and displayed. My class did our project on the Egyptian pyramids. I didn't like that project. It was dull. I wanted to be involved in something more interesting like electricity. The project I stole used a dry cell battery and a bell with a light assembly. It illustrated the power and flow of electricity. I snuck back into school to steal a science project. I took it home and hid it in my dresser drawer. They told the police I hid the science exhibit in my drawer in my bedroom. My mom had no idea I had it. The police came to my house and spoke to my mother. After the conversation they walked right into my room, opened my drawer and there it was. Someone had "ratted" me out. There was nothing I could say or do. I was caught red handed. I knew who told on me, that creep.

This was the first time the police were involved in something that I had done. My mother cried as they took me away. The police took me to the 32nd precinct for a brief stay. I don't know what went on but the final result was that I didn't have to go to court but I had to see a psychologist again. This time I didn't even bother to go.

In the fifth grade I began to run hard with other boys. Mark Stewart was my Brother Keith's friend first. My brother introduced me to him. Keith tells me,

"Walter, I've got a new friend, I've got a new friend!"

"What's his name?"

"Mark! His name is Mark. He hit the teacher in the head with a chair!"

That was bold in those days. So, we became friends. Mark then introduced me to the streetwise boys. Mark lived on 126th and Eight Avenue but he was hanging out on 127th and Lenox Avenue. I met Buster, Ceasar and Lawrence there. Lawrence later became one of my partners and he "ratted" me out. That's another story. But these were the kind of guys whose mothers seemed to let them do whatever they wanted. Not my mom. She fed us, clothed us and expected us in the house at a certain time, but these guys could get away with staying out all night and nothing would happen to them. My mom would wait up for me and when I got in, POW! POW! POW!!! She'd beat me half to death.

So, we'd steal and rob. Rob and steal. We'd hit Woolworth's, W.T. Grant, Blumsteins, supermarkets, wherever. I was an impressive thief. I'd come out loaded down with all kinds of booty. I was skinny so I'd squeeze through small holes and get into stores. We were tearing 125th Street up. We'd snatch pocket books mug men and burglarize stores. It was exciting. I always had something to do. When I wasn't with my brother and his friends I was with the guys from

Lenox Ave. When I wasn't with them I was with my friends from school.

Then something happened. I was eleven years old. I experienced death up close and personal for the first time. The boy's name was Sherman Branch. He lived in the same building in the projects as I did. We lived in building 240. He was in my class. Sherman was eleven years old. He wasn't a bad kid. I was a bad kid, so when Sherman died I asked myself why. He wasn't into the things I was into. He was good. He had everything going for him. So I thought, here I was alive, the little demon, as some referred to me, and Sherman was dead. Dead to me meant you were bad. Yet here I was doing bad things and I was still alive. That was strange. Nothing of any consequence was happening to me. But something was happening. I was being corrupted as my escapades continued.

Two of my best friends in school at the time were James McNealy and William Rainey. Anything that wasn't nailed down after school ended up in our possession. Life continued as usual. Not all of my friends got into trouble. Muscoe Washington, though my friend, never engaged in any of my negative escapades.

I was small for my age as a child. I often passed for being much younger than I was. This was a great advantage during my adventures. My appearance allowed me to get away with many things I did beyond my mother's reach. At the same time I was branded with a curse in the sight of my peers. To worsen the matter I wore glasses, was nappy haired and dark complexioned. It was tough being the butt end of everyone's jokes. All this lent itself to feelings of insecurity. Under certain circumstances I became timid and afraid, especially when being ridiculed and made fun of by those around me.

My youngest sister, Felecia, was born in April of 1959.

I was becoming an effective gambler at both cards and dice. The childhood games of skellies and spinning tops were replaced by flipping baseball cards. Flipping baseball cards led to pitching quarters or playing Pitty-Pat and Tonk for money. From there it went from Bid Whist to Gin Rummy to black Jack to shooting dice. By then it was always for money. By the age of twelve I was arrested twice for burglary and had become acquainted with the juvenile justice system. None of this seemed to affect my performance in school.

When I graduated from the sixth grade I
attended a Junior High school outside of my
district. I was accepted into Joseph H. Wade JHS
117 in the Bronx. The majority of the students
who attended this school were white and all of
them seemed to be better off financially than I
was. I had no problems making friends but it was
known I was not welcome in their homes. It was
not a problem for me because I knew it was
because of my race. After school I would just go
home.

My past time was spent hunting for bottles,
riding the backs of buses for transportation,
running from mean dogs fenced in back yards,
and jumping across roof tops of 8$^{th}$ Ave.
tenements. I was also selling flowers, listening to
stories of stabbings, shootings or police brutality
from the night before, sneaking into the Apollo
and Loew's theaters on 125$^{th}$ Street and flying
pigeons we stole at night from coops in other
neighborhoods from a coop we built on a roof at
126$^{th}$ Street.

In 1963 President Kennedy was assassinated. I was in school on that day. I don't remember anyone saying anything particular to the students, but we were released early. There was a strange silence all around as I went home. It wasn't until later I understood that the President had been assassinated. The next year brought on what the news media deemed The Long Hot Summers.

At the end of junior high school, I was fourteen years old. I had a talent drawing. It was fun. I'd draw cartoon characters, horses, animals, people, trees and comic books. I never thought I was all that good but I enjoyed drawing these things in my spare time. My mother and aunt would encourage me to continue and they felt I had artistic talent enough to go to art school. I was graduating and since my mother said so, I had to go. I forget the name of the school but I knew I had to take an exam to get in. I also needed to put together a portfolio. I hadn't much interest in developing this talent but I liked drawing so I go along. Like I had a choice, Mother and my aunt made me do it.

I get downtown and there were all these students there. They are prepared. They've got their portfolios. They've got stuff! These are real artists. I start looking over some of their work and it's all beautiful. These kids are really talented. I'm looking at the drawings I brought and they are no way as good as what I was seeing. I looked at my measly stuff and I was embarrassed over the quality of my work. I felt I was out of my league.

After a short period we were asked to enter a room to begin the test. When they had given instructions of what to draw I said to myself, "Hey, I don't draw well enough to do these things." They wanted us to draw in spatial content. I didn't understand those terms back then. I do now. They wanted a drawing of a social gathering, a party with people dancing and eating. I couldn't do that. That was beyond my scope. I was frustrated and discouraged. I was defeated before I had begun. I never turned in my work and left before the test was completed.

My heart hardened. I learned to hide my feelings. I became a secretive person. I could truly dislike you and not show it. I could literally hate what you did but hide it. I would smile at you everyday but on the inside care less because I believed you didn't care anything about me. Being forced to participate against my will and being embarrassed made me angry. I didn't know how deep these feelings ran or exactly what they were then. But they had taken hold.

What really happened was I was not prepared for the test. I am sure the proper information was sent to me, but knowing me I either discarded or ignored the material. This would make my disappointment my own fault but my anger wasn't directed at me. Neither was my anger directed at my mother or aunt. I knew they had my best interest at heart.

I knew it was up to me to know what I wanted to do and be willing to do it when the time came. I'd do it alone if I had to.

The times of contentment began to fade during childhood. The residents of the projects were more familiar with the neighborhood and one another. There were bigger, older and sometimes meaner boys outside. New challenges arose trying to avoid being caught by those who would do me harm. If I escaped them, then the hunt for others I could take advantage of would begin. This cycle continued from late childhood through puberty.

At home my sisters, brothers and I all got along well enough. Yet I still remember the many squabbles and fights I had with my older sisters, though my oldest sister, Rebecca, doesn't remember it that way.

Our regular duties were to clean our rooms, bathroom, and kitchen. We learned to do laundry, iron clothes, sweep and mop, take out the garbage, go food shopping and the dreaded wash the dishes. There were always plenty of dishes to wash.

Most of the time I tried to shirk my chores, but that tactic didn't work well with my mother. She was faithful and consistent. If you were given an assignment she would check to see how you were progressing. If you claimed to be finished she would inspect your work. If it did not meet her standards you had to begin the whole job over again. If the work wasn't done right the second time, you gave too much attitude or back talked a well placed lick would set us on the right track.

There came a time I got tired of doing my chores over and over again. I had an epiphany. While doing the dishes I realized if I do them right the first time I won't have to do them again. To my amazement my mother was pleased with the job I had done and I felt good about myself. Each time I was assigned to do the dishes I did the best I could. Before long I found I was required to do the dishes more often than not. This upset me, but I did not complain because the sooner I finished, the sooner I could get out of the house.

My father, Walter Sr., was the strong, outgoing, outdoors type. He loved animals, especially dogs. He also played golf. He kept a set of golf clubs in the broom closet. On Saturdays he would take them out to play. When I was very young his presence was clearly felt. He used to take me fishing and crabbing. I remember us in a row boat out on the water. My hand was in the water as another boat approached. The two boats collided smashing my fingers in the process. For some reason I didn't cry.

I fondly remember him at home mopping and waxing the floors. Boy did our floors shine. Afterwards he would sit in the living room, where children weren't allowed, with his friends talking and laughing, listening to or watching baseball games, smoking his pipe and later his cigars. As his presence began to fade so did our floors.

My father's role was to provide. Once provision was made my mother, Dorothy, took care of everything else from household management to discipline.

Dorothy was an excellent homemaker. Each day she prepared all of our meals. She boiled, broiled, fried and baked daily. She pickled, candied and canned meats, fruits and vegetables. Everyone in the house ate well and many guests enjoyed stopping over around dinnertime to join us. We all ate at the kitchen table together where family prayer was a requirement. Our apartment was always filled with aromas wafting from her kitchen.

Throughout the years various aunts and uncles would come to stay with us for a few months at a time. No one ever explained why they were there, how long they would stay or when they would leave. I believe my mother was just helping them out every now and then.

Dot, as her friends called her was creative and very resourceful. She braided, straightened (hot ironed) and curled my sister's hair. They were always well groomed. My mother knitted, crocheted and sewed. Our apartment was spotless and finely adorned with creations of my mother's inspiration and invention.

There were sugar-stiffened doilies, knitted blankets, quilts and hand made curtains in abundance. She made pants, dresses and skirts, which adorned my sisters and others. All the while my mother was raising us to be respectful of all adults and to mind our manners especially in public. These qualities were easily observed in my mother. My mom labored lovingly, always willing to meet the needs of her children first and to help family members and friends if she could. She was the main ingredient found in the secure and comfortable environment I learned to know as home.

At home I always felt safe. Later as I became more involved in street activities before moving out I would find myself at times in trouble. In those instances my single-minded purpose would be to make it home where everything would be alright. Even until this day my favorite place to be is home.

Like her mother, Weldon, Dorothy was a God fearing woman. She was a member in good standing at Southern Baptist Church Located in Harlem. In my early youth we faithfully attended church together as a family. The boys always had to walk to church while the girls and my mother rode the bus. Sometimes we would race the bus to see who could get home first. Sometimes the boys would win. After church we returned home to eat our Sunday dinner. Sunday dinner was the best meal of the week.  Our stomachs filled with food, we were free to go outside. Of course, if for some reason you were not able to go to church, you would not be able to go out to play either.

My father never attended church, but that did
not deter my mother from directing all her
children to the house of the Lord.

By the age of nine I was a recognized member of
the church. My joining the church surrounded
the fact that my two older sisters were going to
be baptized. Not to be outdone I to asked to be
baptized as well. My mother was so happy that
day over having her three oldest children
becoming a part of the church. After which I was
assigned a deacon and placed on the usher board.
I found it interesting that no one asked me any
questions as to why I wanted to be baptized or
my understanding of the ceremony.

On Sundays my mother sang soprano in the
church choir. She also worked in the kitchen
after service. During church functions one of my
mother's cooked dishes or baked products were
always in demand.

I believe my mother derived much of her strength
from her involvement in the church and the
teachings of Christ. She didn't curse, drink
alcohol, and never smoked. She had a record
collection of Negro spirituals. Often we would
hear her singing or humming gospel tunes as she
worked around the house. At other times the
voices of the popular gospel singers of the day

floated through our house. My mom's favorite was the Soul Stirrers with Sam Cooke.

Due to the lack of my father's family commitment and other weaknesses the mood around the house began to shift. I began to resent going to church. It was so boring. Sitting next to my mother I would become distracted and restless. The next thing I would feel is a well-executed pinch from my mother to regain my focus.

In church there seemed to be this endless request for money, which my mother dutifully responded to. Every Sunday she would make sure we had some change to place in the offering basket, but there was no money available for us during the week.

With my father gone we went on welfare. Every so often we had to stand in the government food line and make a spectacle of our inability to provide for ourselves. This was a very dehumanizing experience as I found myself ridiculed by others who saw you and your family in these lines. Still my mother always had money to place in the church offering. All I could see was a preacher looking very well with his car on Sunday. Why was there money for the church, which didn't appear to need it and not for us who desperately needed it. There was something very wrong.

My behavior became progressively worse and unmanageable for my mother. It was not all that obvious, but my mother knew I was trouble prone. Because of that by the time I was twelve she stopped requiring me to attend church on Sunday to my relief.

## Chapter Two

In his famous 1965 report, Daniel Patrick
Moynihan, then assistant Secretary of Labor and
later a U. S. Senator, emphasizes the rising rates
of single mothers and illegitimacy, divorce and
separation, unemployment and welfare
dependency among Blacks. Unstable Black
families threatened the fabric of Black society in
the U.S. Though this study angered many in
those days, today it does reflect in part a truth,
there was and still is a crisis in the Black family
and the Black community. Though I didn't feel as
if my family was lacking anything but money at
times, I did lose my father to separation.

My father, Walter, and mother were together
until I was about twelve years old. My father
worked in the garment district as a materials
cutter and drove taxicabs. My mother was a
homemaker. After my parents separated or
should I say after my father left, my behavior
worsened. I can't say that was something I knew
then. I do remember feeling like I needed to
pursue my dreams and goals. I knew I dreamt of
saving money to move my mother out of the
projects. I knew I didn't want to be poor. The
absence of my father caused Mom to lose the

greater amount of her financial resources. To supplement the loss, my mother became the provider. She was taking care of six children all alone. That was no easy task. Back then it was difficult for a single woman to get a good job. Job opportunities were far and few between. I know it affected her attitude towards life.

There was a tradition amongst African American urban families of my generation and that was to send your children down South for the summer. We made trips regularly to my father's hometown, Savannah, GA in the summer months. Sometimes my brother and I were sent down and remained without my parents. This happened in 1959 and 1965. During those visits, I discovered there was nothing I could not do or try to get away with doing. Understand that these are the 1960's and the authority we were under was based on race. But we were not swayed by this unspoken rule. Maybe it was our Harlem mentality that gave us this boldness. We were not afraid of adults and not white adults either.

When we'd go into town to the market, we'd steal. The children there were amazed at the audacity we displayed. We'd walk right into the store and walk out with pockets full of stuff. The neighborhood children were afraid because of this unspoken rule of respecting your elders, especially your White elders. They were all "yes ma'am" and "yes sir" and we couldn't care less if an adult was in the room. There were times White adults would speak to me and I'd just walk away. I'd ignore them. This was considered disrespectful but I didn't care. I wasn't afraid of any adult.

Of course, when we'd get into trouble we'd lie. I'd say, " No, Auntie. I wasn't across the tracks at that store. I was out back or down the road." It was nothing for me to lie to an adult. I did, however, get beatings whenever I was found out. My grandfather would lay down the law and my brother and I would stuff our pants with books to protect our backsides. We'd get away with this. We'd pretend as if it would hurt but it didn't. I believe I was a bad influence on the children of Savannah, GA.

The sixties came. Drugs came. I came into adulthood. Though I was a teenager, I was out in the streets in full. Mothers were scared to allow their children to play outdoors. The playground began to deteriorate. Harlem became militant. The sixties were militant. Stuff was going on!

People were frustrated and angry. These were
dangerous times.

People growing older, dying, moving away,
moving in and baby boomers coming into
adulthood became the norm. The sixties were in
full bloom. The Civil Rights Movement, the rise
of the Black Muslims, the emerging 5 Percenters
and Black power was evident everywhere.
President Kennedy was assassinated, then the
murder of Malcolm X. These deaths were
followed by the murder of Medgar Evers and the
assassination of Dr. Martin Luther King. The
Beatles came to America and the music bug bit
many. Sonny, Dallas, Olman and Larry, all
developed a life changing interest in music. Those
who used to sing Doo-op harmony were singing
Rock and Roll. Singers used the echoes in the
public hallways of the projects to complete their
sound while hopeful used benches to develop
their beats. Blackouts, riots, television, the
attitude and behavior of people along with the
face of Harlem were changing. White run and
White owned and run stores began to close. The
last to flee were the owners of stores on 125th
Street, but they too were doomed.

The summer was always a time of anticipation.
There was no school, the weather pleasant. There

was plenty of free time to find things to get into. In July of 1964 riots erupted in Harlem. I sat in my apartment window and saw mobs running back and forth. I snuck out of the house to investigate. All types of people were out stealing. I joined them. The police did nothing. Taking advantage of this liberty I stole all night long and ended up the better materially speaking.

I expected trouble when I returned home. As I quietly entered the house in the wee hours of the morning everyone was asleep. I quietly went to bed. The next morning nothing was said, neither did I say anything.

The civil unrest continued each year. I had grown accustomed to the community eruptions and would look forward to them. In 1965 Malcolm X was assassinated in the Audubon Ballroom in Upper Manhattan. You could cut through the tension in the air with a knife. In the fall of that year New York experienced its first black out and all hell broke loose. People poured out of their apartments and onto the streets.

The looting of the year before was like a trial run. I was better prepared. I am sure everyone did not take to the streets. There were many who didn't move from their residences like my mother, but for every person who did not, there seemed to be two who did on the street. As for me, I was out there smashing store front windows and snatching everything that caught my eye.

In 1968 after the assassination of Dr. Martin Luther King a torrent of rage flooded the African American Community. The drug epidemic had hit the community and many of the traditional moral underpinnings had begun to erode. White establishments were targeted. Their places of business were looted and trampled under foot.

Again I was out there in all my glory. I was a seasoned thug. I knew the back ways and alley ways. We had stash houses set up to store the stolen property. It was all about clothing and electronics. I can not estimate the value of what I stole or the value of the property I destroyed trying to get to what I wanted. Suffice it to say it was a lot.

After 1968 things calmed down in New York. The age of the Long Hot Summers had ended as the counter culture movement that began in the 60's went into full bloom across the nation.

The allure for the streets before the sixties was the number bankers, pimps, conmen and stick up artists. Drugs and junkies were familiar, but they were not popular. Most people avoided them altogether. Initially drug use was contained within the entertainment industry. It was a specialized extra curricular activity amongst adult hipsters.

The Apollo Theater, numerous bars, clubs and after hour spots allowed squares to see the consequences that befell those who indulged in heavy drug use. You could see junkies on 8th Ave. asleep on their feet, nodding until they almost touched the ground. Their arms and legs ulcerous and swollen like balloons. But this also changed in the sixties.

I grew up in this volatile age. I was out laughing, running and fighting. Times were a changing. Black folks had plenty to be angry about or at least they thought so. The sixties were all about speaking out and my teenage generation was not afraid to act on that. I took advantage of this freedom. I had freedom to be vocal and expressive, freedom to pursue whatever desires and dreams I had. I had freedom to be a Black man. So, I took advantage of this newfound liberty and I became more involved in street life.

I knew that I was under sixteen and could not go to jail at the height of my juvenile delinquency. I was also aware of the fact that once I turned sixteen I could be arrested as an adult and go to prison. I told myself I would change at that time and I put forth every effort to do so. I began to go to school more regularly. I curtailed my thievery. I resorted to gambling. My games of choice were Gin Rummy and Black Jack with cards and See Low on the dice.

I was pretty good at both, but like most games of chance you can't always win. What was I going to do? It was easy to think you could stop, but what to do once you stopped was another question. I turned my attention to high school. At the time my hormones were raging as puberty jump-started. In one year I grew 9 to 10 inches. I outgrew everything I owned and my insecurities kicked in.

After elementary school I attended JHS 117 in the Bronx. The school was predominantly White. The Black kids who attended weren't into the things I did and we didn't connect. I graduated and attended my district high school. High school was just a place to be. I found I didn't fit into it. I did not enjoy the academics, neither did I know many people. The lunch period was the high point of the school day. To my surprise the boys would congregate at the back of the cafeteria to play Black Jack. I could see they did not know what they were doing. They didn't even know the rules to the game. Their game wasn't challenging enough, neither did they have enough money. I soon lost interest with the high school crowd.

At age 17 I decided I was going to stay in high school. Many of the boys I ran with like Light and Dark Skinned Charlie, Mark Stewart, Harold Jacobi, Dead Eye Duayne and Nooni either sniffed glue, drank alcohol, smoked reefer, or sniffed dope, but hard drugs were becoming more popular. Teenagers began using heroine for the first time. Up until now I abstained.

Drugs were introduced full scale into the Saint Nick in the early 60's. I first remember One Legged Poochie as the main dealer. He was a legend in the projects. He only had one leg. The rumor was that he lost his leg in a fire when he was very young. As a boy with one leg he stood out. He didn't stand out because he had one leg, but because he was as able as any of us with two legs. He did everything a two legged person did and did it well. He played tag ran races played baseball and road bikes. He also led the charge selling deuces ($2.00 bags of heroine). It was alleged his connect was Ricky Duke another young man from the St. Nick.

Summer was my most favorite time of the year. There was always something to get into and customarily a dice game would unfold at twilight under the lampposts. In the summer of 1967 I broke the game. I won over $1,500 and sent many a hustler home broke that night. High on my luck I didn't want to go home. I eventually ended up on a 129 th Street stairwell with 2 friends, Naheen and Acbar, both into drug use. Naheen was my childhood friend since he moved into 240 in 1959. They pulled out bags of heroine and began to sniff. I joined in.

Periodically I would get high as the occasion saw fit, but drugs were not a major factor of my life. By the spring of 1968 I was skin-popping. I had developed an addiction. I was in the 12th grade and preparing to take the Regents Exam. I met all the requirements for graduation, but failed the English and American history due to poor grades on the Regents Exams.

I went to summer school and passed American History, but failed English. In September I went to register for English. I was informed I could re-take English with 4 other classes. Ridiculous! I dropped out.

I got a job working as an adding machine operator for 57th Street Management. My job was to tally all cab receipts coming out of the Manhattan garage. They had one hundred and one cars for that garage which was their main headquarters. They taught me how to use a three finger adding machine and I was good. I was knocking that work out. It'd only take me a couple of hours to do the work.

There were two other operators there at the time I was hired. I was doing so well they decided to give me more work. I noticed I was the only adding machine operator left. I was making about $65 a week. It wasn't enough. My family is struggling. My mother is on public assistance. I am giving her a third of my money to make ends meet. I am using hard drugs and the rest is spent on carfare. I wasn't making any money. They promised me a raise in three months. So I wait and I work.

I take notice that I can do this job and they like me, too. No joke! These Jewish white folks like me. But I didn't have experience dealing with White folks or adults. In those days, you didn't go near white folks. There was never any racial discussion in our household but there was never any doubt in my mind as a Black child that you don't mess with White people. In regard to adults, you only spoke when spoken to.

So, I know they promised me this raise and I'm desperate for money. Now I'm trying to figure out how to approach the boss. I am trying to get my nerve up the best I can. I definitely was not as articulate as I am now, but I'm going to say what I got to say. So, I go and he says, "Not yet." I was crushed. That turned me against White folks and work forever, but I kept working.

They take me off the adding machines and now I'm responsible for all boroughs and I still have time left over. They teach me the IBM 120 keypunch machine and I'm tallying receipts and doing payroll. They send me to school to learn this keypunch machine and then I'm responsible for doing the keypunch for all of the companies under 57 th Street Management in addition to the tallying. They're cheating me out of money. I'm being taken advantage of now. I believe they're going to do me right because I'm doing right by them. I think they're going to see it and be fair. They take me off of the keypunch and now I'm just responsible for payroll. I get the nerve up again to ask for a raise after eleven months. I'm starving and living hard. Half of the time I don't even have money for lunch.

After getting up the nerve to ask for the raise, they tell me that they're doing me a favor by having me there. "We're training you in computers and this is going to help your future ," is what they said. That did it! I quit. I just walked away one day and never came back. I said I am not going downtown and working for those folks no more. I can steal more than they can pay me.

This was the actual thought I had in my mind because I was a thief. I had been stealing since I was nine years old. I can steal more than they can give me. So, I went to 129th Street to steal and I never went back downtown. That was the straw that broke the camel's back. People were thrusting you into things and not explaining to you what is going on while taking advantage of you in the process. The streets were appealing to me because you got what your hand called for. That's street sense. If you were a punk, you got treated like a punk. If you were bad, you got treated like a tough guy. What you could command you got. I tried this philosophy and I found it worked. It was true. I could deal with that truth. A life of crime proved better to me at the time. I went for broke.

At some point I begin to main-line heroine. I fall heavy into it. Everything up until this time was for fun. It was exciting. Now, I find myself with no money and always in need. I became more violent and aggressive. The older I became the more was expected of me. Without a boyish appeal to hide behind, my lifestyle takes its toll on my family. With no sense of direction anger sets in. I conclude that life is unfair. I can't get a break. To get free, I declare myself a sovereign entity and declare war on everything.

My first serious crime partner was Marvin Carter. He was my age, short and clean cut, but a living terror in action. We were like two peas in a pod. We weren't afraid to try anything. I don't know what happened to him. One day he was gone. Later I heard his family moved out of 255.

My next and best crime partner I ever had during my dope fiend years was Donald Jones out of 237. Unlike Marvin, Donald was just good at thievery and he was tough to boot. We became the best of friends, though we had to keep an eye on one another from time to time. He was the first person to ever come back to help me get away after getting trapped off after a crime. Our time together lasted several months. After which our incarcerations at various times kept us apart. If I was out he was in. When I was in he was out.

In the spring of 1969 I was arrested for the first time as an adult. I was terrified. All the stories I heard came to haunt me. Images of gang rapes and scenes from old prison movies were forefront in my mind. I was prepared for the worst.

The three day bull pen experience is the worst. This is before the time of methadone treatment. If you were addicted to drugs, it was too bad for you. You kicked cold turkey. That was the way it was. You went from the police precinct to the court house bull pens from the court house to the intake bull pens of Rikers Island from there to HDM (Housing Detention for Men). I reached my cell in the middle of the night on the third day.

In the morning I awake to the noise of locks releasing, cell doors sliding open and the incessant drone of hundreds of human voices. In that instant my fears dissolved. I think this is like boys school; I can do this. I was mistaken and it wasn't long before I realized my mistake.

It wasn't those who I didn't know I had to be initially concerned with, but those whom I did know. Besides the shock of that revelation, little harm was done, and after a few days my mother hired an attorney and I was released on bail.

In the prison system it appeared as if Whites did not break the law. On television the inmates were all white. In actuality the inmates were mostly Black and Hispanic. That was another dilemma that life presented to me.

In August my girlfriend, Stephanie, gives birth to my first child, Tesha. After her birth Stephanie and I argued constantly. She wanted me to provide for my daughter and her. I wasn't having any of it. To end the problem I told her I wasn't able to take care of myself. My mother took care of me. If she was having such a difficult time with the baby give Tesha to me and my mother would take care of her too. That severed our relationship and I became an uninvolved father.

I am going nowhere fast. Things came to a head with my mother. For the first time we had a verbal confrontation. I needed some money to get high and asked her. She refused. I attempted to leave the house. She told me I better not. I said," Mom, you never gave me cause to disrespect you. Don't give me one now."

She replied, "If you leave this house don't come back and if you get in trouble don't call me." I left anyway.

I found myself at 19 with no place to go and no prospects. That was no way to be living. I asked myself what I wanted to be. I did not know. I was assured I did not want to be a bum. I answered I wanted to be a man. That night I declared myself a man. I also declared myself a sovereign entity and declared war. If nations could do it why couldn't I? Still with no place to go I decide to go to jail.

On Dec. 13, 1969, I'm arrested for burglary. My crime partner Mark Stewart got away. I had two open cases and was prepared to do some time. I didn't try to contact anyone based on my last conversation with my mother. I was on my own and I was prepared to do what I had to do.

The physical symptoms of withdrawal began shortly after my arrest. Drugs were on the rise and many of the prisoners in the bullpens were going through withdrawal as well. Imagine 10, 20, and 30 at times upward of 50 or 60 men crowded into these large jail cells. When you use heroine it locks your bowels. With no heroine in your system your bowels loosen. There is only one toilet; it usually doesn't work and is filthy. There is no way to relieve yourself. No one has bathed. We are all sweaty and nauseated. We sleep on benches if you have a seat or on the floor using discarded news paper as mats. The food that is served increases the chances of your vomiting just looking at the unappetizing garbage. The stench is unbearable. Each day is the same as you are shuffled from location to location to reach your final destination, 100 Centre Street. If you are not released at court you are remanded to the detention center. There are several more bullpens you endure as the prisoners remanded from all five boroughs are collected together on Rikers Island. On the fourth day you began to recover from withdrawal and your body is restored to a sense of normalcy.

I am jailing now. I don't take any s&*%@# from anybody. I act tougher than I am, but I am determined to be as tough as I need to be. I guess my survival instincts kicked in. I am doing well enough and I keep to myself. A few weeks later I get a visit. It was my mother. I worried her sick. She was glad to see me, but upset because I didn't contact anyone. I was a little confused, but glad to see her too.

My attorney advised me to plea bargain to lesser charges on both cases. Here I thought I was going to go away for several years, but without my saying a word I was offered two six month sentences to run concurrently. I accepted the offer and off to the adolescent detention center, the Quads.

In prison there is no escape. You can't run and there is no place to hide. You either face your fears or you are victimized. Knowing that I was going to prison I made up my mind that jail was not going to break me and if I had the choice jail was going to make me.

Soon after starting my bit the challenge came. Most disputes are over petty discrepancies. A fight was fought and I lost. I retaliated. Forsaking the principle of a fair fight and the fear of the correction officer's retribution I chaired the young man. Amazingly the officers on duty were not aware anything happened and no one reported the incident. After I had that encounter I had no more problems, ever. I settled into doing my time.

The laundry was considered a good assignment for regular inmates. Those who worked there wore refitted starched prison garb. They looked sharp. There were other favored positions like working out doors, in the visiting room or working with the deputy wardens or captains, but I wasn't in the know. I was assigned to the bakery. What made the bakery a choice job was the availability of yeast. Yeast is an essential ingredient for making jailhouse alcohol. You have to be careful making it because it really has a strong odor and is easily detected. Most of the time we were devising means to steal as much as we could get.

After work all that was left to do was play cards, board games or watch TV Another favorite past time was talking about what you knew about crime, women and life. For the first time in my life I was presented with the opportunity and the time to talk to full grown men. And to my surprise they had a lot to say and I had a lot to learn. Some used to say, "Let me pull your coat" or" Let me a drop a jewel on you" meaning they have something useful to tell you.

I treasured those short compact phrases that seemed to have a lot of meaning to how one should respond in life situations. Statements like: What goes around comes around. The cream always rises to the top. You don't get something for nothing. You get out what you put in. The people you meet on the way up are the same people you meet on the way down.

One such conversation rendered a jewel that affected the way I perceived myself and others. Your weight is not measured on a scale. This statement is etched in my memories. It was provided to me by a brilliant man whose name I can't remember, but my understanding of that phrase gave me the courage to stand up to men much larger than I. The idea that no man is an island was also drilled home. I knew that I could not make it on my own, but the grand daddy of them all was 'People take kindness for weakness.'

Sex is a real issue in prison. Many means are devised to relieve that predilection. I totally avoided the booty bandits. Those guys specialized in raping unsuspecting inmates. Those raped and thereby turned out were called sweet kids. I was advised not to take anything from anybody. If someone wanted to give you something, know with a certainty they were going to want something in return. They hovered around the newer inmates testing for weaknesses. They would offer cigarettes and sweets pretending to befriend you. Once under their sphere of influence the pressure would be put on usually enforced with the threat of violence. In the morning after lock out you could see the despair on their faces because of what they had been forced to do during the night.

The next remedy for sexual relief is favoring outright homosexuals. In those days they were called faggots. Most were separated into areas segregated from the general population. I also learned all of them are not scared. Many were capable and willing to knock out those who offended them. Gays in prison live large off the sexual favors they provide. Up state they go all out to display their femininity. Some truly look like women. My release was found in the girlie magazine.

After my release in 1970 I found myself back on drugs and to no ones surprise involved in crime. I didn't much care what people had to say about me. What little conscience I had was relegated to my getting what I believed I needed. Within a matter of months I was back behind bars. I was released and shortly arrested again. I pleaded out my cases and was sent to the Quads.

I had a little more experience on how the system worked and no fear of jail. By the time I returned some of the guys were still there and others had returned like me. I had a strange feeling seeing one of them, a light skinned young man. I believe named Steve in cell block 2. I guess I didn't take jail or crime seriously in those days, but I knew the young man was in deep trouble. Block 2 was set aside for youth facing charges of murder. New York City prisons were over crowded and the courts had mandated the City to resolve the matter. Before I could get comfortable I was transferred upstate.

We did intake at Sing-Sing State prison, the site of the infamous electric chair. I'm a seasoned veteran now and I'm ready to deal. Again I was surprised by what I saw. I expected to see men off their rocker and out of control, a cold brutal place. First I saw plenty of White folks in the mist of everyone else. I remember being led through block "C". As we were being escorted we could look into the cells of the Sing-Sing inmates. Their cells were elaborately decorated. Grown men in their cells totally relaxed. They were reading books, playing cards, checkers and chess. Some were painting and many were smiling. They were intelligent men, literate men. I was impressed. They were all human and they looked like everyone else. I was assigned to Clinton State prison, 13 miles from the Canadian border. On the way up we stopped at Woodburn to drop off the inmates who were assigned to that facility.

I took note of my circumstances after arriving at Clinton correctional. Clinton was real jail; a no nonsense place. All the guards were white and carried these thick batons. There was no doubt that they would be quick to use them if you gave them any trouble.

The inmates of Clinton took themselves and their time seriously. Most dismissed inmates like me who had short time. All types of people were there who had committed all types of crimes. There were men serving 10, 15, 20 years on up to double and triple life. I met men who were behind bars for 20 years. I met men to whom prison life was the only life they knew. They had no hope or desire of ever being released.

Jailhouse rules were different in Clinton. There was an unspoken code of respect; a measure of respect that was demanded if an inmate earned it. If you weren't quick to learn it wouldn't be long before you offended the wrong inmate.

The inmates deliberately segregated the institution. In the mess hall the Whites, Blacks and Hispanics sat amongst their own in specified areas. The same applied to the yard during recreation. Though it was clear these boundaries existed, those lines were not absolutes. Many inmates often crossed over the racial and ethnic boundaries using the primary currency of the jail house, respect.

I was in Clinton when the Attica riots broke out. They shut down the entire prison. We were not allowed to leave our cells for days except in small groups to take showers. Anything else we did in our cells including our meals. This experience forced me to take a more serious look at myself.

I had developed the practice of using my time off the streets to reflect on my life. I asked myself what was I doing thirteen miles from the

Canadian border in a place like this. It was obvious to me that I had to do something better with my life. What was going wrong? I'm 20 years old, one of the youngest inmates in Clinton. I asked myself, what did I want to be? I answered, a man. I asked myself, what I did not want to be? I answered, a bum. Further thought led me to the conclusion that the drugs were my problem. It was after I began shooting heroine that I lost control of my life. I had a $45.00 a day habit. I was only on the street about three months before I was back in jail. To support that habit I had stolen over $10,000.00 in cash and goods. I reasoned if I could steal that much under the influence, how much more could I steal sober.

I thought about my addiction. I could see how my addiction bought out the aggressive nature within me. I liked who I had become. Sitting in my cell I had no urges to use. In the past, the moment I was released the urge to get high joined me. How could that be? I knew I could not have a physical addiction upon release from prison; therefore the urge to use was psychological. That brought an end to my career as a dope fiend. From then on I was going to enjoy the proceeds from my criminal activities.

The rest of my time was spent preparing to take the G.E.D. exam.

I was released and returned to the St. Nick. I was ready. I took my time. I did a job here. I did a job there. It was working. I was staying sober and making money. Then, BAM! I am busted dead to rights for another robbery. It was just bad luck. After the stick up I was making my get away. I wasn't doing anything suspicious. I was pulled over and questioned by the police. As I was being questioned a call came over their radio about the robbery and I fit the description of the suspect. They search me and I'm found with the money and the gun. In the line up, the store manager and the security guard identify me. I am going to jail for a long time.

Back on Rikers in HDM I prepare myself for my stay. I know all the jailhouse regulars, inmates and correction officers. "Hi Walt. You back again." "Yeah. What's happening?" I didn't skip a beat.

I know I am facing a lot of time. I've got a lengthy rap sheet, so I can't expect any leniency from the courts. I could go to trial, but that wasn't feasible. The only chance I had was to learn more about the law and see if I could beat the case on a technicality. I go to the law library and discover what I already know. I have no way out, but I find one hope through the Rockefeller Drug Law.

The Rockefeller Drug Law took a two-pronged approach to address the drug epidemic facing New York. One was to get treatment for the drug user. The other was to put the drug dealer away for as long as possible, even if it was their first offense.

I confessed to being a drug addict in need of treatment. I was informed by my attorney that if a treatment program would accept me the judge would consider my release into their custody.

I started my research and discovered several programs in the Harlem area. I wrote to them all. In a couple of weeks I received two responses. Of the two, I focused on Harlem Confrontation located on 7th Ave. and 121st St.

Now that I had something to work with I pondered over my life circumstances. What was I going to do if I got out? I thought about pimping. I thought about poppin' con. I was already a stick-up kid, so to speak. But I've got to get out of this stick up game because it's out front. Everybody could see what you're doing. That's why I got arrested so many times and I'm catching all of these felonies. So, I know I can't go

57

back to doing this again or they'll put me away for a long time.

What was I going to do? I did not know. I knew I wasn't going to look for a job. The thought didn't enter my mind. I didn't have a change of heart. I just wanted another shot at life on my own terms. I dreamed of getting rich. I wanted to provide for my mother so badly I could taste it. I also wanted to buy her a house, but I didn't have a clue how to make any of this happen. I also needed to get out of the spotlight. What was I going to do? I was longing for a way to make my dreams a reality.

After a few months I was released into the care of the treatment program. I took a dislike to being there instantly, but I had no alternatives. Most of the residents were there because of their parents. They hid behind the staff, their families and their privileges. They weren't serious about facing their problems. Many of them were in denial. They refused to admit to themselves or others that they were dope fiends. They would say things like, "I just like to get high on drugs. That doesn't make me a junkie." If they weren't interested in facing their problems how were they ever going to address them.

I really didn't get along in that program at first. They tried to squeeze everyone into the same mold. I was a very independent person. I always was. They'd try breaking you by giving you privileges, then taking them away. I had a TV while in this program. They took it. It was like a tease. Then they would rank on people and without provocation. They came up with all kind of crap to get under your skin.

I started stealing from the program, but not the residents. I'd rob them blind. I stole cigarettes. Then I'd sneak out and sell them at night while everyone was asleep. They never figured it was me who was doing the stealing. I was always into that kind of hustle. I saw the whole drug program thing as a game. It was just another way for folks to make money.

I met Rose Bayne while in this program. She and I would steal welfare checks that were coming in the mail. She was close to the director of the program, which allowed her access to the mail and I knew Harlem. We'd steal up a breeze. In those days, you didn't need photo ID to cash checks. You could just go to the right grocery store or a bootleg guy and he'd take a batch off of your hands. He'd give you fifty cents on the dollar.

All the residents were required to enroll on welfare. The benefits were mailed to the residence. On check day, each resident was required to cash his or her check and turn all of the money over in the office. That was the last any resident saw of their benefits. We often asked about the money during group. The staff would respond, "That doesn't concern you." They would claim the funds were being used to support our stay there. Everyone knew that was not entirely true.

I was fed up, but I couldn't leave. I had to wait. I needed to stay until I received the final disposition on my case from the courts. I was banking on five years probation.

While at the program I learned a lot about myself. I found out that I was a pretty good cook and I had good organizational skills. Each day the residents were assigned various chores around the residence. It was our responsibility to keep the residence clean and in good repair. The kitchen was one of the most coveted areas for the residents to be. This was not because of the work, but due to the fact that whoever worked the kitchen was allowed to eat anything they wanted. Eventually I was assigned to the kitchen as Ram Rod. This was an important sounding word for the person who had to clean the kitchen and wash the dishes.

We were not a stable bunch of individuals. It wasn't long before the kitchen captain left the program to get high. No one wanted the job as the cook. We had to eat, so I decided to give it a shot. To my surprise I could cook almost anything. Everyone was pleased with the meals I prepared. Not only was I able to cook I ran that kitchen like a well-oiled machine. I believe I learned all of this from my mother. For years I observed her cook and run her kitchen at home. Also to pass the time I signed up to take the G.E.D. test. I scored 286 and blew everyone out of the water. I even amazed myself.

This angered the director because the residents were saying that I was smarter than he was because he had scored 276. It didn't help that I had won the favor of the other residents because of the kitchen. By this time I had been sentenced to 5 years probation. I was overjoyed. The worse that could happen if things didn't work out was for me to receive a 4-year sentence.

My passing the exam earned me more privileges. So, I took the liberty of getting my TV. The program was located down the block from the project I grew up in. So, I went home and picked up it up. I was letting folks use the TV and the staff got mad. They thought I was trying to undermine them, and even though I was, they couldn't prove it. They were upset because I had all of the privileges and they didn't like the fact that they I couldn't just take them away. They wanted to embarrass me.

They tried to take my TV without a valid reason. I told them, if you take my TV I'm going to get all of my stuff and I'm leaving. They said if I did that I'd go to jail. They knew most folks are afraid of jail, but I was not. I knew I could do four years without a problem. I said I'd rather be in jail than to put up with your nonsense. At least you get the respect due you in jail rather than the disrespect you suffer in a place like this. I left.

I knew I was going to get caught and go to jail eventually, but bunk that. They tried to rob me of myself. Naw, I wasn't going for that. I'd go to jail first. I know I went into the program to avoid going to jail. But that was when I was facing 15 to 20 years of jail time. I thought being free would be better, but the kind of abuse they wanted to throw on me…un-uh. I wasn't going to sacrifice my dignity for only four years. Even in jail the COs didn't disrespect you unless you did something to make it difficult for them. But these folk at Harlem Confrontation were trying to mess with my head without knowing what was in it. I wasn't even strung out on drugs in the first place. Yeah I got caught stealing, but I wasn't strung out.

When I received my probation on the armed robbery charge from 1971, I left Harlem Confrontation. I made my initial visit to the probation department. I had no interest in returning neither did my assigned probation officer seem to care if I did or not. I figured I was ahead of the game. I was in jail for six months. I was in the drug program for five months. I was off drugs way before this. Yep, I was ahead of the game.

In the summer of 1971 while in the program I am wide open and game for anything. Ricky Go Go and Poochie Wells are driving brand new 1971 Thunderbirds. One of them had a blue one; the other was driving a brown one. When I saw them in those cars, I wanted to know where they got the money to buy brand new cars. I was aware of drug sales and all that, but I didn't know anything about the money. Matter of fact, Ricky was selling drugs before I went away. He was selling deuces and getting high, but he wasn't making Thunderbird money. It was apparent that there was money to be made and I had to find out how.

I wanted in like I never wanted to be down with anything in my life before. They snubbed me. I was a petty crook and they were big shots. But I knew that anything they could do, I could do as well, if not better. I grew up stealing with these guys. We hung out. As far as crime goes I out did them all of my life.

Before then drugs and drug use were isolated. In the early sixties the deuce ($2.00) bag reigned. There were 15 bags to the half bundle. Those who indulged were confined to designated areas. In the years I used heroine the nickel ($5.00) bag reined supreme. There were 25 bags to a bundle. I was only one of many who fell under its seductive powers. Use of this drug spread like wild fire among the young of Harlem and other areas of New York. Heroine came in along Pleasant Ave. and spread across 116<sup>th</sup> Street from East to West. From there they spread uptown and beyond.

Not only was there an astronomical increase in those who indulged there was a phenomenal decrease of age in those who participated. Young boys/teenagers were out there in mass, participating in criminal activity and drug use. Quite a few dealers were 15, 16 and sometimes younger. It was a sad thing. Before the late sixties young teenagers could not hang out on the avenue much less sell drugs. Adults wouldn't allow it.

It's 1973 and I'm back on the street. I've got to find out what to do to make money. As far as jail goes, they can catch me if they can. 'Catch when catch can', as the saying goes. I owe them four years if I violate my five years of probation. I figure I can do the four years with no problems if I have to.

I was not anxious to go back to jail. I enrolled in the College adapter program. It was located on 125 th Street next to the Loew's Theater. We were in the era of the Poverty Pimps. As a result of the sixties the government through the Anti Poverty Programs released all types of monies into the Black Community to establish community based efforts to help the under privileged. As the name implies the program prepared people for college.

It was said if you could score 310 points on the G.E.D. you could receive a scholarship for college. I figured I had nothing to lose so I retook the G.E.D. exam. This time I scored a 298. I couldn't apply for the scholarship, but I submitted an application to attend City College.

I still needed some money. In any crew you have the hangers on, the wanna 'B's. I couldn't roll with the big shots, but I was respected amongst the wanna 'B's. They told me everything I needed to know. They told me the place they bought their drugs from was called Quarter-land. They were buying quarters and breaking them down to dimes. Quarter-land was anywhere on 116<sup>th</sup> Street and Pleasant Avenue across from Manhattan Avenue. Drugs were big time. You wouldn't believe the amount of money that was being made or the number of people involved. You had to see it to believe it. A quarter cost $60.00 and you could double your money if you broke them down into dimes. The dime ($10) bag was introduced in the early 'seventies.

I was broke and needed the money to cop. I went down to 125th Street, the corner of St. Nicholas Avenue at the subway station and waited until I thought I saw somebody with enough money and robbed them. I went down to Quarterland and bought my first package. I broke it down into dime bags and I doubled my money. I made $240 dollars. It took me two weeks to move my first two quarters. That is a long time to move one small package, but I made $240 dollars. I immediately plunged everything back in and re-upped.

I was engaged in 'hand to hand combat'. That's the term we used for those who sold drugs on the corners. In the beginning I did not have any clients. I had to wait until everybody else finished selling their product. I was the last one on the street selling and only caught the stragglers. The dope fiends didn't know me as a dealer, but they took a chance.

In one week I had over $600.00. In the next few days I cleared over $1,000.00. It was time to go shopping. Leightons was a store on 47<sup>th</sup> and Broadway popular with many who dressed to impress. It was expensive and upscale. For the first time I could afford to do more than just window-shop.

I was excited as I entered into the store. I was greeted by the white sales clerk with a 'what are you doing in here glare'. His words were even icier. I was stunned and uncertain. I was unable to speak and not knowing what to say, I reached into my pocket and pulled out my knot of $1,000.00. As the clerk followed my every move his eyes lit up as he saw the cash in my hand. Instantly his posture reversed with a welcoming and apologetic, "How can I help you sir?"

I don't remember what I bought, but I left the store broke and with a new lesson, the power of money. I knew I was going to sell dope for the rest of my life.

The sixties were all about expressing yourself. My peers and I were nurtured on that philosophy and we were prepared to act on it. I took advantage of this newfound freedom. I could pursue whatever desires and dreams I had. I had freedom to be a Black man on my own terms. I took my freedom and liberty, my dreams and desires and became involved in and committed to the drug life.

Walter and Dorothy Wilson, my parents young
and happily married.

Paternal grandparents- Shad and Rebecca Taylor
Wilson with Uncle Leroy and Uncle Marion as
children, 1921.

Maternal grandmother- Weldon Cunningham

Maternal grandfather- Morris Spicer

| | GEORGIA STATE BOARD OF HEALTH | FILE No. FOR STATE REGISTRAR | B. O. V. S. |
|---|---|---|---|
| 1 PLACE OF DEATH | BUREAU OF VITAL STATISTICS | | FORM 11 |
| COUNTY Mitchell | STANDARD CERTIFICATE OF DEATH | 19743 | |

1 PLACE OF DEATH

COUNTY *Mitchell*

MIL. DIST. NO.

TOWN OR CITY *Camilla* No. _____ ST. REG. DIST. No. *1178* REGISTERED No. *64*
(If death occurred in hospital or in institution, give its name instead of street and address)

2 FULL NAME *George Washington*

RESIDENCE, CITY _____ No. _____ ST. _____ (If not non-resident give City or Town and State)

3 RESIDENCE IN CITY OR TOWN WHERE DEATH OCCURRED _____ Yrs. _____ Mos. _____ Dys. In U. S., if Foreign Birth? _____ Yrs. _____ Mos. _____ Dys.

| PERSONAL AND STATISTICAL PARTICULARS | MEDICAL PARTICULARS |
|---|---|
| 3 SEX *M* | 4 COLOR OR RACE *Col* | 5 SINGLE. MARRIED. WIDOWED. DIVORCED. *Married* (Write the word) | 14 DATE OF DEATH *Aug 1st* 192*7* |

3 SEX *M*   4 COLOR OR RACE *Col*   5 SINGLE. MARRIED. WIDOWED. DIVORCED. *Married* (Write the word)

5a IF MARRIED, WIDOWED, OR DIVORCED HUSBAND of (or) WIFE of

6 DATE OF BIRTH, (MO.) _____ DAY, _____ YEAR _____

7 AGE *85* Yrs. _____ Mos. _____ Dys.
IF LESS THAN 2 YEARS   IF LESS THAN 1 DAY _____ Hrs. _____ Min.
State if breast fed. Yes _____ No _____

8 OCCUPATION
(a) Trade, Profession or particular kind of work *Farmer*
(b) General nature of Industry Business or Establishment in which employed (or) employer

9 BIRTHPLACE (State or County) *Va.*

10 NAME OF FATHER *D.K*

11 BIRTHPLACE OF FATHER (State or County) *D.K*

12 MAIDEN NAME OF MOTHER *D.K*

13 BIRTHPLACE OF MOTHER (State or County) *D.K*

14 THE ABOVE IS TRUE TO THE BEST OF MY KNOWLEDGE.
(Informant) *Garfield Washington*
(Address) *Camilla Ga.*

16 FILED *Aug 15* 192*7* *OO Worley* L. R.

MEDICAL PARTICULARS

14 DATE OF DEATH *Aug 1st* 192*7*

17 I HEREBY CERTIFY, THAT I ATTENDED DECEASED FROM _____ 192*7* TO *Aug 1st* 192*7*
AND I LAST SAW H_____ ALIVE ON *Aug 11* 192*7*
AND THAT DEATH OCCURRED ON THE DATE STATED ABOVE AT *10* A.M.
THE CAUSE OF DEATH WAS AS FOLLOWS:

*Senility*

(DURATION) _____ YRS. *6* MOS. _____ DYS.
CONTRIBUTORY (Secondary)
(DURATION) _____ YRS. _____ MOS. _____ DYS.
WHERE DISEASE WAS CONTRACTED, IF NOT AT PLACE OF DEATH
DID OPERATION PRECEDE DEATH? *No* DATE OF _____
WAS THERE AN AUTOPSY? *No* WHAT TEST CONFIRMED DIAGNOSIS? _____

(SIGNED) _____ M. D.
(*Aug 15* 192*7*) (ADDRESS) *Camilla*

19 PLACE OF BURIAL, CREMATION OR REMOVAL *Bethel Cemetery* DATE *8/14* 192*7*

20 UNDERTAKER _____ ADDRESS *Camilla Ga.*

Great great grandfather George Washington's
death certificate. Husband of Amanda.

73

Top photo- Corrine, maternal great grandmother
with great great grandmother Amanda holding
grand aunts and uncles.

Bottom photo- Grandmother Weldon
Cunningham

74

Dad and Mom in Savannah, Georgia as teenagers

Shad Wilson, standing in front of the house he
built.

# PATERNAL FAMILY TREE

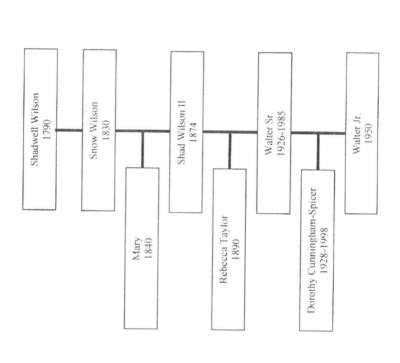

Shadwell Wilson
1790

Snow Wilson
1830

Mary
1840

Shad Wilson II
1874

Rebecca Taylor
1890

Walter Sr.
1926-1985

Dorothy Cunningham-Spicer
1928-1998

Walter Jr.
1950

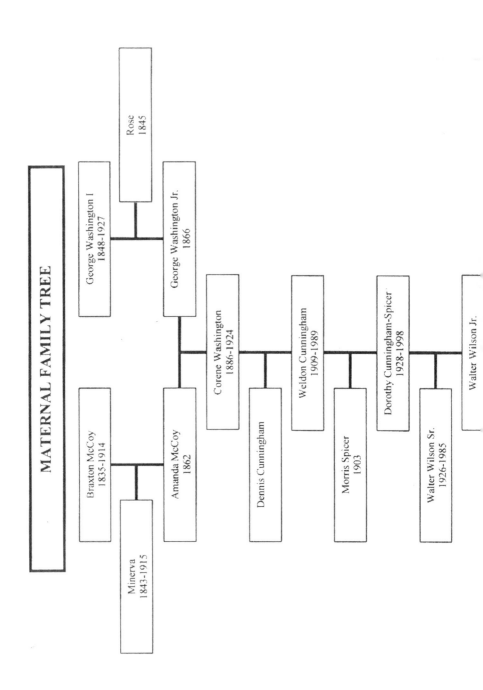

# MATERNAL FAMILY TREE

George Washington I
1848-1927

Rose
1845

George Washington Jr.
1866

Braxton McCoy
1835-1914

Amanda McCoy
1862

Minerva
1843-1915

Corene Washington
1886-1924

Dennis Cunningham

Weldon Cunningham
1909-1989

Morris Spicer
1903

Dorothy Cunningham-Spicer
1928-1998

Walter Wilson Sr.
1926-1985

Walter Wilson Jr.

78

Mom, Dorothy Wilson, married and in New York

Dorothy, an industrious woman

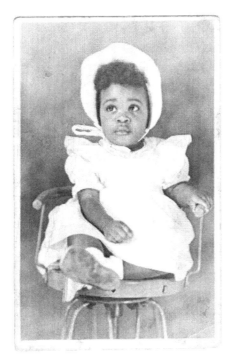

Top- Dorothy's icy wagon
Bottom- Rebecca Jean Wilson, their first born

Top- Growing family, Betty Theresa, new addition

Bottom- Still growing, Walter Wilson, new addition

82

These pictures represent our move into the St.
Nicholas projects.
Top- The children on a trip

Middle- The construction of the St. Nicholas
Houses

Bottom- The children in our new apartment, 240
W. 129th Street, #5G, the St. Nicholas Houses.

Top- My parents out with friends
Bottom- Birth of Keith Randall Wilson, I'm
behind the stroller.

First family portrait, 1956.

THE CITY OF NEW YORK
## DEPARTMENT OF HEALTH

125 WORTH STREET
NEW YORK 13, N. Y.

TEL. WORTH 2-6900

Sept. 8, 1955

Mrs. Dorothy Wilson                    Re: Walter Wilson
240 West 129th Street                      7/1/50
New York 27, N. Y.

Dear Madam:

    We are holding all papers relative to filing a
delayed birth certificate.

    Through a telephone conversation with the Cor-
respondence Office of Metropolitan Hospital, we were informed that a new letter was mailed to you, giving the correct birthplace of the child.

    Kindly submit the letter to this office, so that
we may file a delayed birth certificate and issue a copy to
you.

    We are enclosing an addressed envelope for your
convenience.

                            Very truly yours,

                            William Stern
                            Borough Registrar, Manhattan

FS/mg

Correspondence letter for birth certificate

THE CITY OF NEW YORK

# DEPARTMENT OF HEALTH
BUREAU OF RECORDS AND STATISTICS

125 WORTH STREET
NEW YORK 13, N. Y.

Date _____ Sept. 13, 1955

Dear Sir or Madam:

You recently filed an application to record the birth of       Walter Wilson which was not registered at the time of its occurrence. This application has been approved by the Commissioner of Health and the birth certificate has been placed on file in the                office of the Bureau of Records and Statistics under Special Number   1bo-55-b41 491 .

In view of the fact that the application was accompanied by a "Not Found" statement, issued in response to a request for a search of this birth record, a certified copy is sent you herewith.

Very truly yours,

CARL L. ERHARDT
Director of Bureau

By _____ _____ _____

Letter confirming issuance of birth certificate
Letter confirming issuance of birth certificate

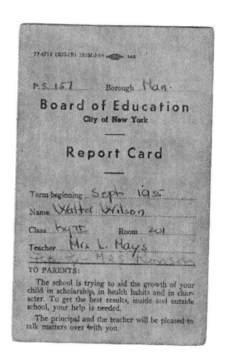

Kindergarten Report Card

Kindergarten class picture

89

First grade class photo

Second grade picture

BOARD OF EDUCATION
CITY OF NEW YORK

Public School  *157*            Borough  *Man*

## REPORT TO PARENTS

### GRADES 4-5-6

September 19 *60* - June 19 *61*

Name of Pupil  *Walter Wilson*

Class  *5-1*                    Room  *401*

Miss-
Mrs.
Name of Teacher  Mr:  *Laurie Ferris*

Dear Parents,

The purpose of this report is to tell you how your child is getting along in school. You will receive reports three times a year — December, April, and June.

No two children are exactly alike. This report is about the growth of your child.

You are urged to make comments in the space provided. If you have any question, please feel free to arrange a conference with your child's teacher. Please sign and return this report promptly.

Cordially yours,

BERNARD FRIEDMAN
Principal

**Ratings Used**
Exc.—Excellent
Good
Fair
Unsat.—Unsatisfactory

Fifth grade report card

92

Top left- Mom and dad

Top right- Dad with children, Darryl Curtis
Wilson, infant

Bottom left- Keith, Darryl and baby Felecia Avis

Bottom right- Dad with cigar and Mom, still
together.

Family portrait #2

Top- Informal family portrait at home

Middle and bottom- Family on their way to
church

Top- Coney Island outing 1960's
Bottom- Walter Wilson's sixth grade graduation

96

Sixth grade class picture

BOARD OF EDUCATION OF THE CITY OF NEW YORK

JUNIOR HIGH SCHOOL ___117___

BOROUGH OF ___Bronx___

## REPORT TO PARENTS

_Wilson, Walter_

Pupil's Last Name     First Name     Middle Initial

_Sept, 1963_     _8-127_

Term Beginning     Official Class     Home Room No.

_B Flessig_

Official Teacher

The work of the school is planned to discover and to develop your child's aptitudes, abilities and interests. Cooperation between home and school will contribute greatly to your child's success. The principal will be pleased to confer with you.

First Report—Teacher's Comment

I have read this report _Dorothy Wilson_ 11-18-63

Parent's Signature

Second Report—Teacher's Comment _Walter's gradby baby_
_fallen off in the second quarter. More_
_effort is necessary. Poutty self control_

I have read this report _as required_ _Dorothy Wilson 2-7_

Parent's Signature

Third Report—Teacher's Comment _Walter's behavior_
_has shown little improvement_

I have read this report _Dorothy Wilson_ 4-9-64

Parent's Signature

Fourth Report—Teacher's Comment

I have read this report _____

Parent's Signature

NEW OFFICIAL CLASS ___9-132___ ROOM _____ DATE _____

TRANSFERRED TO _____ HIGH SCHOOL DATE _____

Eight grade report card

98

THE LOUIS D. BRANDEIS HIGH SCHOOL
145 WEST 84th STREET
NEW YORK, N. Y.      10024

MURRAY A. COHN,
PRINCIPAL

TO PARENTS OF CANDIDATES FOR GRADUATION

DEAR _Mrs. Wilson_

    The report card of your child _Wilson, Walter_ of class _8-5_

shows failures in the following subjects:

    English 8       A H II
    B & Y        H. Ed.
    D & 3
Most failures are caused by absence from class or lack of homework.

You can help your child to pass by reminding him to do his homework and making

certain that he goes to school on time every day.

                    Yours truly

                    _____

                    Senior Grade Advisor

Trouble in school

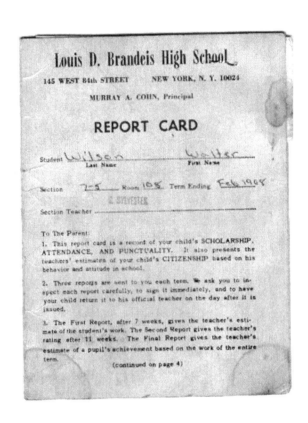

## Louis D. Brandeis High School

145 WEST 84th STREET      NEW YORK, N. Y. 10024

MURRAY A. COHN, Principal

## REPORT CARD

Student Wilson                    Walter
        Last Name                 First Name

Section 7-5 Room 105 Term Ending Feb 1908

Section Teacher _____

To The Parent:

1. This report card is a record of your child's SCHOLARSHIP, ATTENDANCE, AND PUNCTUALITY. It also presents the teachers' estimates of your child's CITIZENSHIP based on his behavior and attitude in school.

2. Three reports are sent to you each term. We ask you to inspect each report carefully, to sign it immediately, and to have your child return it to his official teacher on the day after it is issued.

3. The First Report, after 7 weeks, gives the teacher's estimate of the student's work. The Second Report gives the teacher's rating after 11 weeks. The Final Report gives the teacher's estimate of a pupil's achievement based on the work of the entire term.

(continued on page 4)

High School- 12th grade report card

100

Top- My brother Keith Wilson

Middle- Keith with friends at home

Bottom- Darryl out with friends

101

Growing up
Top left- 14 years          Top right- 16 years
Bottom left- 18 years          Bottom right- 20 years

102

Top- High School "non-graduation" photo
Bottom- Stephanie Mance and my daughter        Tesha

Top- Walter and Felecia      Middle- Walter and Betty
Bottom- The Wilson siblings

Final family portrait, 1974

# Chapter Three

Like everything else you have to learn the ropes if you are going to succeed. What were the dos and the don'ts of selling drugs? I understood how to be a thief, but selling drugs is new to me. Financial security appeared to be the solution to most problems. I was looking to avoid being lonely, bitter and impoverished in life, especially in my later years if I could live that long. What I had seen of adults didn't inspire me to desire a long life.

Things got going fast. I am feeling real good about myself and my prospects are looking up. It's time to pursue the American dream. I believe I have the means to become financially independent and make my mother proud.

Developing my own philosophy was not only necessary for my survival; it was essential for perfecting my business style. I was in this hustle, all or nothing, for life. I was determined to rise above those I grew up around and the imagined limitations super imposed on me. I had to make money. I longed for a sense of satisfaction and accomplishment along with the symbols of success that seemed to be at my fingertips. I had to have the car, the clothes and the girl.

I trace my awareness for my need for a woman to age 15. It was a pleasant day weather wise. I was with 2 acquaintances, Cleveland Bumpers and Aubrey Anderson. We were leaving 125th Street after coming into some money. As we walked along 8th Avenue pleased with ourselves I asked, "What are we going to do now?"

"We are going to our girlfriends house," was their reply. "You can not come. You don't know anything about that." I wasn't wanted. As we continued to walk I slowed my pace and fell behind. They didn't even seem to notice. As I turned into 129th Street I swore to myself that no one would ever do that to me again. LESSON: Always have a girlfriend. Until then I understood sex to be taboo.

The music of Motown and Atlantic records educated me in my relations with women. The Tempting Temptations, Aretha Franklin and the Isley Brothers, "It's Your Thang" provided the directions I followed. I was under the false impression girls didn't like sex. I was in shock to learn how easily some girls shared their bodies. Many times I found them to be the sexual aggressor. It took me a while to figure out that girls gave up sex for different reasons than I accepted it. I accepted sex because I liked it. It

107

seems they, because they were looking for something more from me than just sex.

When I left the program in 1973 I went to live with my mother. She was always there for me. I loved my mother and was always respectful of her. That's the way she raised us. My mother was not aware of what I was into at this time, but she was suspicious. After she would leave the house I would bring the fellows in to prepare our product for the day. On this one occasion she doubled back. Maybe she forgot something or maybe she laid a trap that I got caught in; I don't know. All I know is I looked up and there she was in the doorway of my bedroom. No one heard her keys jingle; the front door open or her foot steps down the hall. I was caught. All around me were fellow crooks, and piles of white powder on an album cover. I had gone too far. It was one thing for me to venture into criminal activity; it was another to expose my mother to it. It was time for me to go. I collected my drugs, my crew and a few things and left. By the days end I had my own place. LESSON: I would never expose the unwilling or innocent to my dealings in drugs, especially when it comes to my family.

Selling dope came easy to me. There was money to be made everyday, but all days were not the same. In spite of heroine's reputation most users were not destitute street people. Yes, heroine is destructive and if given time it will erode your life as statistics evidence and common sense dictates, but most users are working people. Many others use recreationally.

For lower level heroine dealers more money is made on Fridays and Saturdays than any other day of the week. After the weekend the money slows down and slowly picks up steam as the week progresses. Sunday is called the dead day. Few people come out to hustle and even fewer come out to cop. People just disappear.

One Sunday night in late 1972 I am bored. It is unseasonably warm out side. To occupy my time I start gambling under the lamppost in the projects. I only have $600.00 in my pocket to re-up and enough money to pay my rent. In the heat of the moment I roll the dice and lose all my money to a chump that luck favored. LESSON: Never gamble with your drug money. Only gamble with money you can afford to lose.

I was surprised by the amount of deaths that occurred amongst those in the drug game. I made it my business to understand why. There turned out to be three main reasons men died in the streets: money, women and mouth or any combination of the three. LESSON: Don't mess with people's money; don't mess with another man's woman and don't threaten anybody. If you are going to do it; do it. This understanding led to the most important thing; take care of yourself and don't die in the street!

There was too many who did not live up to that rule. Many died before they reached the age of thirty. Here is a list of some of them.

> Shorty, Snoggy, Cooder, Puss, Lover, Ronald Parham, Jonathan Spell, Janet Johnson, Albie, Magilla, Niecie, Pug, Darryl, Russel and Freddie Woodard, Butch Byrd, Tyrone, 'Don', Napoleon (Nopo) · Lorenzo Anderson, One Leg Poochie, Bobby, Girl Bobby, Blind Mike, Butch and Linda Bracey, Authur, Puggy, Saladine, Peabody, Omar, Tom, Knappy, Ty Roscoe, Chuck and Ray McNealy, Crack, Cleveland Bumpers, Allan Janette and Lil' Johnny.

Seventeen of them just wasted away. They overdosed; others died in freak accidents and the untimely deaths of the rest from lifestyle related health issues like hepatitis. The other twenty-one were flat out murdered. At least one was killed by the police, and another committed suicide. Most of the others were killed over money; women or they were too tough for their own good.

There were only two other major tenets in my philosophy: you only go to jail for making money and no snitching. LESSON: Jailhouse reputation and personal character is necessary to survive.

I had to get to know the opposition. I had to be aware of the foot patrolman, the patrol cars and the narcotics detectives. It was important to be aware of all the officers regularly assigned to the neighborhood. Some days the police were all over the place. On those days it was best to go home. On other days they were nowhere to be found.

Other patterns watched were the movements of the police. Who was working what shift: 8 to 4, 4 to 8, and 8 to 12. This took time to understand because for the first 6 months after the summer of 1972 I was on 8th Avenue everyday selling dope with a host of others and we did not see one police officer. We were as green as unripe apples. In that time no one I knew was arrested or even stopped and questioned by the police. You saw the daily passing patrol car, but that was all.

I believe to this day that a conspiracy was hatched. The understood plan was to allow drugs to flow unabated in the urban centers of America for a season. The conspirator's goal was to undermine the social concessions won in the Civil Rights movement and the Radical 60's. It was a bold attempt to hinder continued social progress by diverting attention from positive activity to self-serving and self-destructive behaviors. It worked.

Cops were not my biggest problem. If you lived outside of the law you had to be on your "P"s and "Q"s for those who also broke the law. I had to be on the alert for the tough or slick dope fiend, wanna be gangsters, stickup men and other drug dealers.

Most of the young drug dealers were new to the streets. They were just coming out of the house. They were experiencing freedom for the first time. I watched as good boys turned bad overnight and become totally corrupted and depraved. They were not fully prepared for the consequences of their behavior. They assumed this was the way it was always going to be and the consequences were inconsequential.

Many of the guys I hung out with as a boy did not make the transition. They exhibited potential in their early childhood and youth, but by now they were addicted to alcohol, strung out on dope, morally bankrupt, intellectually deficient, or spiritually broken and filled with fear.

Many of the dope fiends were good people who got caught out there. They fell into drug use as a recreational pleasure that ultimately consumed and perverted their lives. They did not possess enough personal resolve to pull back when things began to get out of hand.

Out of these ranks came my greatest challenges. Life was a rat race. Dog eat dog. The laws of the jungle prevailed. Only the strong survive and Darwin's survival of the fittest applied.

The Illusion was complete. I, along with all the rest, threw caution to the wind. The allure of a false sense of freedom and the free flowing dollars were too good. They were intoxicating. We were functioning in our own world clouded under an atmosphere of delusion.

In those days we dressed to impress and we stood out like neon signs. We were all color coordinated. If my color of choice for the day was brown, I would wear brown from head to toe, even my shades, socks and underwear would match. Leighton's and A J Lester's on 125th Street were making a mint. I had sneakers in every color to match the outfits I chose to wear. The more prosperous had a car or two to match.

We were ignorant to the fact that we announced to the police who we were and what we were doing. All this was superficial, but important to us at the time. Live fast and enjoy the moment, no wonder we were being harassed and arrested by the police regularly once they began to appear.

Drugs were also color coded to identify your product. There was Red Tape and Blue Tape. There was Green Tape and Double Green Tape. As time went on and more people became involved the variety increased. Dealers walked around with knots in their pockets totaling 2, 3, or 4 thousand dollars. Most of the money belonged to your connection for re-up. The point was not who the money belonged to, but the fact that you could command that type of money that did the trick. I liked hustling and I was getting good at it.

I made crime look good. The younger guys in the projects saw what was happening and were lured into the snare of glamour and fast money.

By the summer of 1973 I was fully immersed in the drug game. I was small time selling hand to hand. Those in the know called it the asshole end of the business. I had no arrests and was making a comfortable living. Rose Bayne, the girl from the program, and I were shacking together. Our

relationship was a disaster. She was pregnant
and I had no time for a family. My focus was on
the streets. To make matters worse she began to
use again. I was going to get rid of her. It was
just a matter of time. I stayed in the College
Adapter Program because I wanted to complete
something positive and an education couldn't
hurt.

Now that I was supporting myself I set out to
find my father. When I was younger he hung out
on 145 $^{th}$ Street between 7$^{th}$ and 8$^{th}$ Avenues or on
133 $^{rd}$ Street between 7 and Lenox Avenues. I
did not know any of his friends, but I knew they
called him Cavanaugh, Oyster or by his first
name, Walter. I thought that we could do
something together. After three days of searching
I located him at a woman's house on 141st Street
and 7 $^{th}$ Avenue. After speaking with him I
realized we were not going to click. There were no
ill words or sentiments between us, I just
understood what I had in mind couldn't work for
him. After further inquiry I decided the only way
I could help him was to buy him a car to use as a
gypsy cab. I bought him a 1970 American motors
sedan. I gave him a few dollars to get started and
went back to what I was doing. After that I did
not see much of him.

I dealt on 128th and 129th on 8th Ave. I was aware of all the neighborhood regulars. I knew the residents, merchants, police and dope fiends. Using a sharp eye and even sharper instincts I was always on the alert for strangers lurking on the block. If there were any they were usually under cover cops or stickup men.

I was bold and fearless. I would walk up and down the street and verbally broadcast the brand I was selling. I made no attempts to put shade on any of my activities. I would often stop and confront the strangers in the block. I would size them up and make my pitch.

One particular day was different from the rest. It was a special day. As was my habit, I observed 2 men standing in a doorway. They stood there for some time watching the goings on in the block. Suspicious I approached them. "What's up? What are you doing here? Do you want to buy some drugs? I've got Double Green." I stated. They shook their heads and didn't say a word. I didn't know these guys at all, but they seemed interested in me. I took them for stick-up kids and stepped off.

Another kid I grew up with who was well connected was on the block named Jellybean. As

116

I was leaving he approached me and said, "Some guys down the block want to see you."

I replied, "What these guys want to see me for? They want to buy some dope?" I was thinking this was a set-up and my tone suggested as much.

Jelly had moved into the St. Nick in the late 50's or early 60's with his mother. He was about 10 to 12 years old at the time and the only child living with his mother, though he had siblings who were grown. His real name was Stanley Green and he was game for just about anything. One of my earliest memories of him is his standing on the stoop of 240 eating jellybeans. Ronald Gilliam, another youth of the St. Nick asked him for some of his candy and Stanley said no. Ronald from that day on began to call him Jellybean and the name stuck. Everyone called him Jelly and most never new his real name.

Jelly and I became close friends. That friendship survived until the invasion of drugs and our fall into that lifestyle. Most friendships from my youth did not survive the foray into drugs and on this day my trust of Jelly was in question.

Jellybean replied, "No Walt it ain't like that at all." He insisted that I had to meet these guys. So, I decided to see what was up. It was Guy

Fisher. I didn't know him personally only by reputation, but my conduct had impressed him.

Guy wasn't new to the game and he had come up through the ranks fast. He was from the South Bronx near Third Ave. He was also reputed to be one of Nicky Barnes' top lieutenants. Nicky Barnes was the most well known of the larger than life drug dealers in Harlem during that era.

Guy asked, "You want to sell drugs for me?"

"Who are you?" I said.

He said, "I'm Guy. Do you want to sell drugs for me?"

I replied, "OK, I'll check out what you got."

"Meet me at Coney Island, twelve midnight," was his response.

The other man with him was James Brown, a close friend who grew up with Guy. He was back up.

Coney Island was a pool hall in Harlem on 126th Street and Seventh Avenue. So, I show up at midnight and Jellybean came with me. When Guy arrived again with James Brown they open up this box full of dope, which had to be about five hundred bundles. I never moved anything like that. I move two to five bundles a day, tops.

He gives me the package and I say, "Man, I can't take all this dope! Give me some, let me go sample it, then I can tell you how much I want to take."

So, he gives me two bundles for a sample. That's five hundred dollars for me. I go out and I sample it and folks are telling me it's a monster. So, I come back and I tell him, "OK, I want the drugs, but I can't take all of it."

He gives me twenty-five bundles and I move them in short order. I figure I'll go back to him and I tell him I could get him people who could move his drugs for him. At the next drop off I ask him if he wanted me to do it? He says, " Yea." And just like that I'm in.

Recruiting was easy. I went to 8th Ave. and pulled half of the projects. I brought them up to a bar called Club Alabama on 140 th Street and Third Avenue in the Bronx. There must have been about twenty of us. We're there and we're waiting for Guy to show up. When he does, he pulls me to the side and tells me to handle all these guys. That's when I became big and I started to expand. It literally happened overnight. I gave them all some dope and for a little while I had the run of Eight Avenue. I had established a good standing with a major distributor. Let the big times roll.

I registered for my college classes in the fall. At first it was interesting, but my life on the streets was a major distraction. Things were going well for a time and as luck would have it my troubles began. Murphy's Law kicks in. From December 31$^{st}$ 1973 to January 16$^{th}$ 1974 I caught three cases. I had one felony possession and 2 observation sales. I got out on bail on all of them. I've still got five years probation hanging over my head and any day the warrant is going to drop and the police will be looking for me for that. Soon after, I later learned, I caught a case in Washington, D.C. for selling drugs to a guy out there. It wasn't really my case, but I didn't know it at the time. This ended my college career.

One of the most difficult things for a distributor is finding trustworthy dealers and keeping your crew stable. In the beginning I was able to keep up with my workers, but to add to my grief I began having problems with my crew. My stress level began to increase along with my cocaine use and violent behavior. This was when I found out Rose was shooting up. I could not believe how stupid she was. Not only was she stealing drugs from the packages I was delivering; she was getting high while pregnant. When confronted she vehemently denied everything, but word had gotten back to me from those on the street. Because of what she was doing many of my workers were beginning to complain about receiving short packages. I think I'm being played and become more aggressive and then physical. It's very dangerous for you once you become physical. It is even more so if you are in the wrong.

Angel Dust hit the street. We called those who smoked it Dust Heads. People started losing their minds. Dust heads were jumping off roofs, jumping out of windows and getting hit by cars.

That was the beginning of the breakdown of many of my childhood friendships. Many I knew, knew of my girl's drug use, but didn't inform me because her behavior benefited them. They put my life on the line for their own selfish needs. A deep sense of distrust of others began to settle in.

So, I got these cases. I begin to consider the potential consequences. I had a felony possession and two sales plus my four years for violating probation. There's a law that says for sale of drugs you get life imprisonment. This is part of the Rockefeller Drug Laws. It was reasonable for me to assume that I would be going away for ten to twenty years. Ten to twenty with life on the back is a long time.

My cases began to make my connections nervous. Fear is a dangerous commodity on the streets. Sooner or later someone would suspect that I would cooperate with the police and trade me for them. To get off their radar I began to operate on a cash and carry basis only.

Because things were not looking too good for me at the time, I decided not to return to court. Bunk it! Catch if catch can. If this was going to be my last hoorah I was going to give it all I had. I was going to have as much fun and make as much money as I could before things caught up with me. I left the streets and ran stuff from an apartment I had up in the Bronx with another woman I had named Maria. I went into full time distribution.

Before I went into hiding I convinced Rose to go into the hospital to detox. In March of 1974 she gave birth to my second child, Lamar. I knew I was going to go to prison eventually and the life of his mother had spiraled out of control. Neither of us was in any condition to raise a child. I was concerned. The only solution I could envision was to ask my older sister Betty to step in. Not only did she agree, she raised him as her son and selflessly provided for him for the rest of his life.

I remained on the run for eight months before the police found me. It was my arresting officers, Manetta and Ironmocassin who apprehended me. I wasn't expecting them, maybe officers from the warrant squad, but not them. Before my final arrest I had a couple of close calls, but I got away. It looked as if I wasn't going to be as lucky this time.

I was captured as I came out of my apartment building on Teller Ave. to buy some chicken noodle soup. I was frozen. I was skeeted to the gills. I mean I had sniffed too much cocaine. I began to snort cocaine like it was going out of style. It had become a daily occurrence. I came out and I didn't have on a shirt. I had just thrown on my coat and shoes. I had no socks and had just a couple of dollars in my pocket for the soup. I had more than thirty thousand dollars in my house. I had little money, no drugs, no gun and no one else was implicated in my flight from justice. It was just me, caught crossing the street on my way to buy some chicken noodle soup.

They took me to jail. But, I was relieved. Living on the run was hard on me. It was stressful like you wouldn't believe. I asked the officers how they came to suspect where I was and officer Manetta informed me he looked over my bail applications and saw that a person who had posted my bail lived in that area. On a hunch they decide to cruise the neighborhood. I congratulated the police officers on their good police work and shook their hands. The officers later told me they thought when they caught up with me that I would be strapped and carrying. On any other occasion that might have been true.

At 100 Centre St. officer Manetta smiled and said to me," We've got you now!"

I told them, "No, this is just round one."

I know the ropes. Fear and ignorance are no longer governing factors for me. In the American judicial system you are innocent until proven guilty. Your arrest is round one. Your court negotiations or trial represents round two. Round three is your sentencing. I didn't know it at the time, but I was going to utilize all my legal rights.

It's ironic that I was able to learn and understand a lot about people during this period between my incarcerations. Most importantly I learned we all were human beings trying to do the best we can with what we understood we had. The police were only people trying to do their job.

I learned if you respected them your time in their company would be less difficult and amazingly they would respect you as well.

I understood that no one expected criminal activity to end in the legal arena. What was being done was performed to manage criminal activity and to prevent the most atrocious acts from taking place and to keep the worse criminals off the streets.

The radical sixties had come and gone and with the sixties went the Negro. The underbelly of the American system was revealed. America was a racist nation. In the Land of the Free the colored were second-class citizens. The African American was unjustly treated on every level. We were systemically and systematically excluded from full participation in the liberties other ethnic groups took for granted. In the end this meant you could not trust White people or any of their institutions.

Naturally, I rejected the Euro centric stereotypical portrayal of Black people. A brief study of the history of America revealed the dishonest, immoral, unethical and corrupt practices that authorized the dehumanization of other human beings through the institutions of slavery along with the colonization of the world by other western European nations. Those practices secured the prosperity, growth and prominence of the United States. This was criminal activity on a national and international scale. Forget the endless babble on the benefits of moral character. Forget honesty and truth, decency and merit, good or bad. Why was good, good and bad, bad? I was no longer willing to consider the doctrine, do good in this life and when you die you receive happiness in the life to come. What about now? How do you attain happiness now? I was not open to accepting a supreme being who was sovereign over all things in life. Who could prove if that was true? I knew that here and now was real and that was good enough. I decided I would deal with everything else after I die.

True history revealed crime and criminal activity are a means to an end. It inferred you could get good from bad, right from wrong and peace from turmoil. This was the way of the world. If nations could employ deceptive and unjust methods to attain glory, so could I.

# Chapter Four

Back on Rikers I was gearing up for my stay. To what lengths was I prepared to go? I knew to take my mind off the streets and to focus on matters at hand. One of the toughest ways to do time is to dwell on what's going on in the streets. A many an inmate suffered mental breakdowns because their bodies were in prison, but their minds were on the streets.

I immediately resorted to the laws of survival: self-preservation and survival of the fittest. I was going to look out for myself. As I stood on the second tier of block six looking down onto the flats, I realized that everyone I saw was just like me. From that vantage point it seemed to make perfect sense that the best approach would be to look out for everyone I could if I was going to effectively look out for myself. I dropped the defensive attitude and put into practice the concept of, one-hand washes the other, but both wash the face.

Upon resolving my immediate need I began to evaluate my present state. I knew I was a man of respect and had won the admiration of most and the envy of others. Why was I able to bear up when so many others folded? I reasoned by basic abilities derived from my upbringing and the discipline I received from my mother. A hard head makes a soft behind was one of the many words of advice she would dispense while I was being whipped. My mother did not spare the rod. I was beaten often when found in the wrong. She taught me early that there were consequences for doing wrong and if caught be prepared to suffer those consequences. Don't complain because you should have known better. I translated her advice to mean, if you can't do the time don't do the crime and you don't cry over spilt milk.

Secondly, why was I able to resist heroine addiction and the fate that had befallen many I had grown up with? I reasoned that my earlier arrests and often incarcerations familiarized me with kicking cold turkey and staying sober at least until I was released. Beyond that while jailed my peers maintained their freedom and addictions. They were accustomed to getting high and staying high. Their self-demoralization had left deeper scars on their psyche, making it harder for them to resist their shame and making it easier for me. Lastly, being jailed so often increased my street reputation, therefore a higher expectation was anticipated of me by my peers. This gave me more to look forward to and thereby a greater sense of self-esteem.

I further reasoned that crime did pay. The question became, how come I made so much money? I wasn't the smartest or toughest guy around by a long shot. Yet, people sought me out. I concluded it was because the people I knew and worked with could trust me. I was willing to sell drugs everyday, 24 hours a day. My resume' was ideal for crime. I was a known criminal dating back to my childhood. I had several adult arrests and several bids under my belt. I never folded or snitched and most importantly I always paid for my packages and took responsibility for myself. I was a distributor's dream.

In the past the most I could expect was a visit or two from my mother. This time I was in for a pleasant surprise. Before my final arrest I was living with Myrna in the Bronx. She was a little older than I was and deeply involved in the streets for a good portion of her life. She was well connected and respected. During my days in hiding she was able to represent me when I was unavailable. She had a keen understanding of what to do if troubles developed and she was loyal.

Myrna was able to maintain my drug enterprise for a good period after my imprisonment. She made every court date and made visits 2 or 3 times a week. She kept me in money and the latest fashions while I was away. She also retained a lawyer for my defense. Any attention you get from the outside boosts your persona on the inside. My stock was going through the roof.

I turned my attention to my cases. After my arrest all my warrants dropped. I was going to court 2 and sometimes 3 times a week. With all those charges I was preparing myself for the worse. The Rockerfeller Drug laws mandated that I get life attached to the end of any sentence received. The best offer made to me was 6 to life for all my cases. Others around me advised I should take it as they took plea bargains with life sentences on the end. I figured life was too long even for a guy like me. I didn't believe I deserved a life sentence. I also knew I wanted to try my hand again as a criminal. That would be very difficult having a sentence with life on the end. That would give the police carte blanche in arresting me and prevent me from making bail in the future if I was ever arrested because of a parole violation. Finally I thought six to life versus ten to maybe fifteen to life if I lost at trial wasn't a big difference. I felt it was worth it to me, to take the risk of receiving an additional four to nine years if I went to trial.

I discovered over the years that the legal system functioned on the fear, ignorance and poverty of most inner-city defendants. It fed off of the defendant's fear of being in jail any longer than he has to, his ignorance of the legal system and the lack of resources at his command to compile a proper defense. I was going to learn as much as possible about the law and court procedures that bound me to my crimes.

Another advantage was the prosecutor did not know all the aspects of my case. He was drawing conclusions on the evidence at hand especially that of a co-defendant who had turned states evidence on me. Knowing this I was prepared to testify and tell my story, as I knew it to be.

Many talk about going to trial, but few do. The few who do are either in denial or are facing so much time that they would receive the same sentence either way. All eyes turned to me as I announced I was going to go to trial. And they continued to watch as the process unfolded.

remained on Rikers for sixteen months. I had been through a riot, tear-gassed and saw officers charging in shielded in riot gear busting skulls as they went to regain control of the facility. After order was restored I played Bridge on my down time. After all was said and done, I had been to trial twice, received hung juries both times, submitted a brief that made the Law Journal and finally received a four year sentence running concurrent with any and all outstanding cases. I had won the day. The day I struck the final deal with the prosecutor I became the envy of the incarcerated criminal element. All throughout Myrna was ever present.

I was sent to Fishkill Correctional after my intake at Clinton Correctional to complete my sentence. While there a brief was submitted on my behalf for my release. While incarcerated I read constantly. I read books and authors such as James Allen, As a Man Thinketh; Machiavelli's The Prince; The Prophet, by Kahlil Gibran; The Auto Biography of Malcolm X, History of American Robber Barons, American Gangsters, La Costa Nostra, Ann Rand and much, much more. As a hobby I created glass paintings. (I finally found a use for my artistic abilities.) To further my education I took advantage of the college courses available at night. I passed with a 3.2 average. In the afternoon I took and completed a shop course on internal combustion engines. I finished top of my class.

After twelve more months I went to the parole board and was hit with the remainder of my sentence. That same week my brief was approved and was I immediately released without ceremony.

With my newfound freedom I had a package on the streets in three days. I was not about to become a member of someone else's crew. Before going away I sensed my well being jeopardized because I had open cases. I read too many signs that reflected the fear, uncertainty and questionable trust that other dealers had for me. It would not have been the first time someone was eliminated because their people considered him a threat.

If I was going to do this, I was going to put together my own crew and work independent. Buster and Mark Stewart, childhood friends, were my main support. The preferred method I employed was cash and carry. I would purchase drugs from any number of dealers. I was always on the lookout for the best deal. My minimum was double your money. If I spent $10,000.00 I had to be guaranteed $20,000.00 in return.

It was like I had not been away. Of course there were many new developments. Guy Fisher and his crew all caught cases with the Feds. Nicky Barnes was serving life and would soon turn states evidence on Guy Fisher et al. I was thankful I caught my cases earlier in the decade with the state. If not I surely would have gotten swallowed up with Guy in his legal troubles.

These events formed the basis of a theory I surmised. There seemed to be a pattern of ten years allowed for whoever was at the top of the drug trade if they could survive, give or take a year or two. Nicky had his decade, Guy his decade and I thought that I was a good a candidate as any to fill the void that was about to be created in the streets. I was going to have my decade.

I thought I was ready for this major expansion. The quality of my incarceration and the man I represented myself to be opened doors for me. While away I met many men who were steeped into the drug trade. Men like Mikey Barrett, Sweat Pea, Peanut, Bobby Miles, Vincent Hunter, Stevie Monsanto, Fat Bobby White Boy and others at the top of the business.

On the other end of the hustle I established relationships with men from the Bronx, Brooklyn

134

and Queens. These guys knew their neighborhoods and wanted to give dealing a shot. Men like Lefty, Black, Ron and Robert. I was already in with those from my neighborhood and all my connections from before my arrests that were still around: Calvin, Joe, Sonny, Crab, Indian, Flats, Spider and more. The greatest dope peddler I ever knew on 8$^{th}$ Ave. was Eggie. Boy could he sell dope. No matter how much dope you gave him. He would move 100, 200, 300 bundles a night. I was always looking to give him a package.

I already believed you could only fully rely on yourself. No matter how many people you had working for you something was bound to go wrong. To protect myself I established a base of operations on familiar ground, 8$^{th}$ Ave. I needed to identify a location off the street that I could control to sell my product. I needed a hole in the wall.

The idea was spawned in me by an old dope fiend named Jack. Jack ran a shooting gallery out of an abandoned building on 8$^{th}$ Ave. There were many abandoned buildings in those days and more were becoming available each day.

One day Jack approached me for a package. Jack was the dope fiend I brought my samples to when

I first met Guy. He also touted for me on my first package of twenty-five bundles. I knew you could never trust a dope fiend and Jack was a dope fiend from the old school. That old fiend continued to plead; assuring me he could move as much as I could give him. Against my better judgment I gave him a two-bundle package to shut him up. In less than an hour he was back for a re-up.

Curious about how he did it. He told me to follow him into the abandoned building. Alert to the possibility of a set up I cautiously followed him. On the third floor in an apartment in the back he had a shooting gallery. The apartment was filled wall to wall with junkies getting high. Here was this old dope fiend off the streets and out of the eyesight of the police selling dope to a command audience. I gave him a larger package and he became one of my most reliable dealers.

It wasn't long before I had located a brownstone on 8 th Ave. and 127 th Street. I made a deal with the owner and set up my base operations there. I now had my hole in the wall. I allowed another dope fiend to run the gallery named Jabar. He was from the St. Nick and in times past he was someone to reckon with on the streets. I set up the preparation room, the stash room, and the room to sell the drugs and watched the money roll in. It was a gold mine.

There is always someone you have to deal with because of ego, envy or jealousy. Most of the time some type of confrontation was required. I never liked going physical, though I would fight if I had to. Most times I didn't have to fight. There was usually somebody around me willing to take someone on. It was not like I commanded them to. It was more like my being a natural leader. Folks would always follow me. Those inclined to be physical would just step up. If I had to fight, someone would say to me, "I'll take care of this Walt. You hang back." It was a symbiotic relationship. I would look out for folks who ran with me. I made sure you got what you needed. It was like that. I would want somebody to do it for me like that. But it was me, I was the idea man. I was a talker, the one who understood. I made the money and divvied out your share.

This guy named Sheppy hated me. Suffice it to say I didn't like him either. We never got along. He wanted to be a gangster. He wanted to be a hustler, but he didn't have it in him. He just had anger. For me he was new to 8$^{th}$ Avenue. When I came home from prison he was there. I came off. He didn't. One day he walked up to me and said,

"I need some work." I wasn't giving this guy anything and I let it be known in no uncertain terms. He got hostile. So be it. It's time to fight. So we square off in the street.

Before anyone could swing a blow Mark Stewart stepped in. He said, "I'll take care of this." My problem was solved. I began to realize who I was on the street. There were a few who did not like me, but I had a cadre of respect from other folk who were willing to risk there lives to preserve mine.

I was still on parole and I wanted to keep it that way. It turned out my parole officer was ok. I was required to make weekly visits at first. His name was Fieggenbound. He advised me to get a job. There was no way I was going to look for work. I told him I was going to go to school. Of course he did not believe me. His final advice to me was, "Don't show up for a parole visit driving any brand new cars or having a pocket full of money." I took his advice, though I did enroll at Pace University for a semester. I majored in Business Administration. I figured if I made enough money I could use the information I learned to go legit.

In the first year I took micro and macro economics classes along with marketing. In the economics classes I learned that the national flow of money is tracked by the central banking system regionally. Whenever too much money begins to flow into any region, financial policy is adjusted to redirect the money flow along a more desirable direction.

It appeared to me that if too much money was being made in North Eastern urban areas the central bank would adjust its policy and cause money to flow into other areas. That was an unfair manipulation in my mind.

In advertising we were informed that the average American reads below a $9^{th}$ grade level. All marketing promotions are designed to appeal who read below the $9^{th}$ grade level. In my naiveté I felt the marketing industry should edge up the reading levels of their marketing promotionals to assist in propelling people to higher levels of comprehension. My professor didn't agree.

Over all the halls of higher learning was a disappointment to me. I thought I wasn't being taught how to create and run a business. I was being taught how to manage someone else's business. I passed all my classes, but when I finished my parole I didn't return to college.

It was not long before I ran into Detective Mannetta on 8th Ave. When he saw me he pulled over. I was clean and didn't have anything to fear, though I preferred him not to see me on the Ave. He asked what was I doing and I replied nothing. He looked me up and down and I could tell from the knowing look he gave me he was aware of what I was up to. He didn't say another word. He got into his car and drove away.

The accumulation of the symbols of success began. But first I wanted a woman to share it all with. My relationship with Myrna had turned sour. Women were always trying to control you. They start out sweet, loving and understanding then, bam; the switch-er-roo. Since my previous relationships turned out badly I thought getting a younger woman would allow me an opportunity to avoid the defensive and sometimes offensive shield women seem to put up because of their bad experiences with other men. Boy was I wrong.

At this time in my life women came easy. Most were attracted because of what they heard or saw of me. These were not the type of girls I took seriously. They couldn't see me for who I was, only for what they could get. What I needed was a main squeeze. She would be the woman who believed in me for who I was. She would be my personal possession, not as in chattel, but as someone I could always count on for anything and she would desire to do this willingly. For me a Black woman was the only thing a Blackman could fully trust in this white world to be your own. White folks are always changing the rules to everything to maintain their unfair advantage in life.

I found my main squeeze in the person of Diane Thomas. She was a good friend of my youngest sister Felecia. I knew her and her family from the time we were children. The Thomas family was one of the original St. Nick families. They were there from the beginning. At first they lived in 240 in apartment 6B. After their family size increased they moved to 225. Diane's older brother Ricky was a good friend of my younger brother Darryl. Ricky was never formally involved in the streets. He preferred sports and excelled in basketball. Later in life he fell victim to the crack epidemic from which he has recovered.

Diane was seventeen and she was no stranger to me. I believed I could work with her. I was not into the practice of using women in the street to hustle. I preferred them to go straight and be free of crime and my drug business in particular. I needed my woman to be above suspicion. Diane wanted all those things as well. I didn't believe she would pose any major relational problems.

Compared to me she was a baby girl. I called her my 'Baby Girl'.

By the summer of 1978 it is time to get rich. I buy the gold, the diamonds, the clothes and the car. The object is not to remain a criminal forever. In my attempts to go legit I open a furniture store, variety store, start a cab company and purchase real estate all at different points. My attentions always remained on the street. My hope was that these enterprises would be successful and then I would be able to shift my focus to them and maintain a comfortable living. It would not be so.

All of them failed miserably. It was impossible for me to find trustworthy help. It seemed to me that honest people were more dishonest than us crooks. If you dealt with crooks you knew what you were dealing with, but with honest folks, they say one thing and do something entirely different. Things never turned out the way they said it would be.

On my down time I hung out on Lenox Ave. and 128 th Street in Al Sapp's spot. Next door in the Old Colony a boyhood friend, Buster Darby, hung out. This was Buster's neighborhood. Buster was my partner. While I was away he ran numbers on Lenox Ave. He was never one to go to school, but you would never know that by the way he handled himself. He had a sharp memory and did all types of mathematical calculations in his head. More importantly he had a good heart and he was no push over.

In Al Sapp's the fellas boasted and talked nonsense. We gambled and sniffed cocaine. Cocaine is an expensive habit. I discovered I was losing money because of it. I began to sell cocaine out of my hole in the wall. I used the profits from my cocaine sales to support my cocaine habit. Things were going so well I was sniffing $1,000.00 worth of cocaine and losing $2 to 5,000.00 on a given night playing Knock Rummy in Al Sapp's.

I was at the top of my game. I was a successful criminal. Most of the people I knew or associated with were like me in on way or another. It was those people who made up the core element of those who hung out at night.

On the street more dope is sold on Friday and Saturday than any other days in the week. The same similarity appears on the weekends in the after hour dens. To my amazement things began to pick up around Thursday and by Friday Al Sapp's would be jumping. Friday is when the eagle flies. Friday is the day most people who work get paid. Out came schoolteachers, postal workers, transit employees, janitors and sanitation workers. These were the working stiffs. All of them were seeking to join with the men of the streets. Their desire was to gamble, sniff, flirt with the ladies and wine and dine with the rest of us. We were their idols. To them we were men of adventure, taking all sorts of risks to survive. We were their heroes, men facing life on life's terms and coming out ahead. We made them feel better about themselves. It was glory by association.

How was it that the supposed good people were looking up to bad guys like me? This was not the way things were supposed to be. No matter, I did not have the time or inclination to concern myself with it. If that was the way they were playing themselves, they would get what they had coming to them.

As men we forget very easily that we received all sort of help in becoming successful at what we do, unless we are constantly reminded. Ego seems to set in as greater success and feelings of independence unfold. Once entertained these feelings allowed me to believe I was doing or had attained my success all by myself. I was

144

beginning to forget. Everything was seemingly going my way.

The final feather in my criminal cap came in the summer of 1979. A block party was taking place in 128 th Street between 7th and Lenox Aves in schoolyard of P.S. 68. It was a perfect summer day and everybody was out. As I am enjoying the festivities I see this guy William Bryant out of the corner of my eye. He is not aware that I see him. I give him time to pass by me. Thinking that he had passed by me unnoticed, I observe where he had obscured himself. I took a hammer out of my trunk, snuck up behind him and assaulted him with the hammer.

Don't ask me what I was thinking, but everyone was aware that I had assaulted the man who had betrayed me in public. My fate was sealed. From then on many spoke of me in hushed tones. I enjoyed the notoriety and basked in the aura.

In the morning I would frequent my base of operations. By now the spot practically ran itself. I kept it well stocked with rubbing alcohol and new syringes. There was a $2.00 charge applied to anyone for the use of my facilities. The place was clean and comfortably decorated. I would never announce when I was coming and of course I would try to be as inconspicuous as possible.

The idea was to blend in and go unnoticed especially by the police. Gone were the neon days of my beginnings. The spot was run in shifts. I took the morning, Buster the afternoon and Mark Stewart the nights.

The spot generated 3 to 5,000.00 dollars a day plus an additional $600.00 made from addicts who used the gallery. I was in my glory. I was the man. Everything was working out just like I wanted them to.

In time I became a bigger drug user than any drug fiend I sold heroine to. A junkie would spend twenty to a hundred dollars a day to support their habit. I would spend two to five hundred dollars a night to support my cocaine habit. I began to realize that I was no better off than those I sold heroine to and society looked down upon. My outlook was beginning to change. I had attained what I had always desired and had worked towards. I had a run; I was on the streets for more than a year making consistent money. Yet I was not truly happy. I was stuck in a rut.

Every attempt at legitimacy failed. I could see I was surrounded by the dregs of society. Until that day I never saw myself as a bad guy, even though I led a life of crime. Liars, cheaters,

146

thieves, murderers, whoremongers and more were my constant companions. We were all these things and it wasn't a stretch for us to do this stuff. These things were inclusive in our everyday actions. It's hard to believe the stuff we were really into. Worse still I was at the center of it all and more often than not I was the ringleader. We would be sitting around and someone might say, I've got some static. Everyone knew what that meant. Someone else would pop the question," How are we going to do this?" An answer would come and we would be off.

Or someone would come in and say, "I know this one or that one and they've got twenty G's or some drugs in a stash. Let's go take him down." That's how we were living.

I lost a sense of accomplishment. Where was my sense of satisfaction I expected in my success? I was still a top predator, but I was also preyed upon. I was losing my edge. My perceived success preceded me. I had made money for too long in street time and those on the prowl saw me as a mark. If I was caught unawares all there would be is the predator and I. No police. You get your 50/50 chance. You cannot expect better odds than that in a fair game. I always walked with both eyes open. Now I did not have enough eyes to see every angle.

I was alienated from my family. Their love for me was unconditional, but my life-style was alien to them. I often walked with concealed weapons. My life was always at risk. My freedom could be lost at any given moment. It was best to keep my immediate family at a distance. This was proven one afternoon in 1978. I was on 8th Ave. when I spotted my mother walking towards me. Before she could reach my location an under cover police car pulled up. The police jumped out and arrested me on the spot. The horror on my mother's face filled me with great sorrow because she was forced to see this happen to me. Nevertheless I beat the case. They couldn't find any drugs nor did they find any marked money. This was my life on the streets.

By 1980 I had impregnated three women. Each gave birth to one of my three children. My oldest child Tesha was seven years old when I was released from prison in 1977. She was living with her grandmother. Her mother, Stephanie Mance, was stabbed to death while I was incarcerated. During a moment of self-reflection I was hurt to realize that I had not spent more than $200.00 on her during her life. Yet I would spend hundreds if

148

not thousands on gambling and getting high daily.

I also noticed my sister Betty, who was a professional in accounting and worked for the Board of Education, was living comfortably with her husband and family. As far as material possessions go, she had everything I had without the grief and misery.

I had gotten the younger woman, Diane. She was not involved in the streets and I kept her out of my dealings. Still it was impossible for me to protect her from the daily dangers I faced and accepted as a way of life. This was a great source of worry and aggravation for me. By 1979 Diane and I were having problems. We are fussing and fighting and in those days it was real fussing and fighting.

In my dealings with Diane I rejected the idea of women being 'sugar and spice and everything nice'. There was no sugar there was no spice. Well maybe sometimes. Diane was still a teenager. Where was the sugar and spice? There was something more sinister at play in the hearts of women. I reverted to a masculine philosophy. Something less complicated and more straight forward. If a man were to hurt me physically or emotionally I would hurt him in return. If you are man (woman) enough to dish it out you have to be man (woman) enough to take it. This what Diane would get from me.

That didn't work either. Men respect strength. The women I have known didn't. I have experienced them coming at me with all they have knowing full well I am going to hurt them. Yet still they come. That didn't make any sense. My actions didn't help. They did not solve any problems and they did not bring us any closer together. Things just got worse.

I presented a cavalier attitude. If things don't work out with one woman, drop her and get another. So, I left Diane for another woman. For the first time I felt grief over my actions. I felt responsible for her. I took her out of her mother's house and introduced her to my version of independent living. I was unfaithful and immoral. What could I really expect? I learned that the hard way, women are not disposable.

Toward the end of 1979, it was put upon me to count the money that I had made in the past year. I began to realize that I would never get rich. I was good for about three to five thousand dollars a day. Just walking out of my house I could make three grand. So, I'm calculating this stuff, and when I'm finished figuring and deducting my overhead I had made over a quarter million dollars cold cash. That is a very conservative estimate. Yet, at the end of the year I had $7,000.00 in cash, three cars, a bunch of jewelry, clothes and a package valued at $25,000.00 on the street. Where was the wealth? What happened to the money? What was wrong?

Other views I possessed were also challenged. I saw in retrospect how I had changed over the years. I was a totally different person in 1979 from the one I was at age sixteen coming into this drug life hard and heavy. I was no longer the young, wide-eyed, innocent man who began this criminal journey at the age of 16. I lost my innocence. I had lost a lot. I had lost my humanity over the years. I could see I was a cold, hard, calculated individual and could actually do the worst of things to people and myself and have no qualms about it. I was trapped in a life-style of wickedness with no way out. These thoughts and many others presented to me the inevitability of my circumstances. My understanding of my sense of self was breaking down. There was something beyond my learned frame of reference eating at me. I needed to keep these realizations to myself or all would be lost.

Freebasing became popular. Some I knew at the top of the game who smoked coke lost control of their operations. They started messing up packages, abusing themselves and abusing others. They started losing money and eventually losing touch.

As things might have it my troubles began to worsen. I began to lose it, so I thought. In fact that was not the case. I survived by my wits and instincts and they had to be sharp. I believed those traits allowed me to stay a step ahead. I believed once those qualities were tampered with I was doomed. Soon thoughts I could not control began to enter into my mind. Fear and uncertainty began to creep into my heart. I began to question my behavior and my motives. Something was messing with my internal being. I was no longer comfortable with myself or within myself. I feared I was losing my grip. My perspective of what was going on within my spot, within the conversations going on and with regard to the dangers I faced was changing. I was afraid.

My mind was on violence. Guy and his crew were convicted and he was sentenced to life imprisonment. The void was evident. If I was to come out on top I had to make a move soon. One of my most disappointing discoveries was that at the top of the ascending order of drug-life were white people. They were at the top running everything. We as African Americans were still just second-class citizens. I also recognized that of those of us who were killed in the game for the most part were killed by other Blacks. It was not the police. It was not whites. It was us killing one another basically for nothing. It was too late I was trapped in a life-style with no way out. I was beginning to think I had messed up my life. These thoughts and many others presented to me the inevitability of my circumstances.

All of these new thoughts and changes were taking place. What was going on? I did not have the answer. Under all of this my delusion dissolved. I was crushed. I was lost. I made a few feeble attempts to reach out, but was scorned. A sign of weakness is the surest way to death; so, I did not persist in revealing my vulnerability.

There came a point one night while I was laying up snorting cocaine and feeling miserable, and as an act of desperation I cried out for help. I did not pray to God because I was not sure of Him. If there was a God he had not proven Himself to be on anyone's side. To me He was obviously distant and uncaring. The only recourse I had was to ask,

"I don't know what is going on, but if there is anything good out there come and get me." I had a sincere desire to get out, but I had no place to go.

# Chapter Five

In November of 1979 my spot was raided. I was sitting in my usual seat in the front of the room at a desk near the window. From my vantage point I could see everything coming up 127th Street from 7th Ave. I didn't allow anything to get into the building unless I saw it first. Nothing would come through the door or into the room where I sold drugs that I could not deal with.

As I peered through the window I had a sense that the police were coming that day. I was totally prepared. I said to everyone in the room, "Get ready, we are going to jail today." I was confident everything was going to be all right. Within an hour the police came in like storm troopers.

In raids like these the police had a practice of letting all the women go and keeping the men. Today was no different. They lined up all the men and had us face the walls. We were searched and they confiscated all the drugs and drug paraphernalia. No one had anything incriminating on their person. All the incriminating stuff was recovered off the floor in the back of the room. Everyone made sure that they were as far away from the stuff on the floor as possible. Outside the paddy wagon awaited us once we exited the building handcuffed and in single file.

During the ride, and our relatively speaking brief stay in the court bullpens, I constantly reassured those arrested that everything would be all right. All they had to do was keep quiet and let the process take its course. I knew only those with warrants needed to be concerned. If their warrants dropped before we reached the judge they would be remanded. All others would be set free.

There were about fifteen men arrested at the time of the raid. Of those fifteen four or five had warrants. The rest had the charges dismissed and were set free. This was routine procedure and it worked like a charm. I already knew the outcome. I had a sense of being above the law.

When I returned to the neighborhood I went to my spot to survey the damage. As expected the police had destroyed everything they touched. They left the rubble strewn throughout the rooms, but this time something unusual had taken place. As I looked over the damage I saw a Bible on the floor. I remember thinking, what is a Bible doing in here? I knew that there were no religious people in my place of business. At that moment I heard a voice in my mind say, Walter, read the book. You know so much about everything, but you don't know much about God. Pick up the book and read it. That made sense to me, so, I took the Bible home along with my cocaine and tried to read the Bible.

I had more difficulty trying to read the Bible than I thought I would. At first I tried to find familiar passages like The Lords Prayer, The Ten Commandments, Turn the other cheek and the lord is my shepherd. I couldn't find anything familiar. I did not know where to begin. I didn't even know that The Lord is my shepherd was the opening line of the 23$^{rd}$ Psalm. In my frustration I heard a voice say, read the book like a book. Start at the first page and read it to the last page. It was brilliant. That revelation made perfect sense. I began to read the Bible like a book. So here I am snorting cocaine and reading the Bible like a book.

The Bible I recovered from my spot after the raid was a large print New Testament King James Version (KJV). By the time I had finished reading Matthew through to the book of Revelation I had a desire to read the Old Testament. Many of the passages in the New Testament relate directly to the Old Testament. To get a clearer understanding of what I had read and the nature of God it was without a doubt necessary to read the Old Testament.

Earlier in the year Diane and I spent some time at a Pocono Mountain resort. We went away to spend some time to ourselves. In the room was a Bible placed by the Gideons, which I took when we left. That Bible contained both the Old and New Testaments. I located that Bible and began reading the Old Testament from Genesis. It took me nine months to complete the entire Bible from Matthew to Malachi the first time. I was in no hurry. I read it carefully. The book was amazing. By the time I had completed reading the entire Bible I had come to know God and believe in Him.

Some of the things I read in the Bible were hard to accept or difficult to understand. I knew it was impossible for me to perform some of the things the Bible seemed to require for my life. Other things that were written came across very clear. At first this posed a problem for me. After I thought about it for a while I decided not to worry about what I could not understand and focus on what I could, and see what happens. As I learned to accept and practice what I could understand, understanding would come in areas I previously had difficulty accepting or practicing. This became an ongoing process. Striking balances  in all I learned was necessary.

During the nine-month period I continued to have difficulty maintaining control over my thoughts and feelings. Something continued to mess with what was inside of me. Something was going on that was changing my perspective on what was happening in my life and about the behaviors and conversations taking place in the gallery. I was losing my heart (a sense of fearless confidence) and at times I feared I was losing my mind. My perception of the daily risks and dangers I faced flipped. This was different. This wasn't the wary cautious attitude I used in the past. It was cold fear.

I battled daily with this interference. I struggled to keep my sense of control and to maintain my composure. I was trying to figure it out. I needed to have a sense of confidence and control to survive in my environment.

The dope fiends started looking at me funny. My partners were looking at me funny. They were trying to figure out what was happening. I'm saying things like,

"Do you hear that? Do you feel that?" I was hearing and feeling strange things.

In the past my partners and I were in sync with each other. I had a feel for everything happening in my space, but now I can't connect, I am off the page. Here I am selling drugs and I am feeling things, I am hearing voices. I think someone is talking to me, but there is no one there. I am trying to take care of my business. I ask myself, what's wrong with you? I'm hustling trying to make sense of what I am reading in the Bible and figure these things out in my mind. Every day I go home and read my Bible; the next day I come back and sell my dope. Each day I would psych myself up and try to push everything out of my mind except what I had to do to keep my operation running smoothly.

One day I'm speaking to Buster and a few others about what was going on in my mind. A dope fiend who overheard the conversation butted in and said, "Walter, that's God speaking to you and if I didn't tell you God would be angry with me."

I didn't know who this guy was nor did I expect any understanding of my dilemmas to come from a dope fiend. Yet it began to make sense. All the events of 1979 and before were part of a move of God on my life. God was speaking to me. He was trying to get my attention. No one else I had spoken to during this time even remotely understood what was happening to me. If what the dope fiend told me was true, it was revolutionary. God speaks to people directly. Even more astonishing, if true, God was taking the time to speak to someone like me.

Could this be real? Is there a spiritual realm that exists and overshadows the material realm? Was God really speaking to me and calling me to Him? Could I dare believe that my experience was somehow unique? Where was the human intervention? Was Christ interceding in my life by His own spirit? Here I am at the height of my criminal activities and on the cusp of reaching my goal and He enters into my life. He did not enter through the window or doors I guarded so fiercely. He invaded my mind and entered through my heart. Why?

This was strange and so weird in and of itself. My best belief was if God did truly exist, He existed unto and within Himself. I didn't even consider that God was actively involved in life and He existed within everything that is. Grasping the reality of God being omni and ever present was going to require some major concept adjustments on my part.

I began to see how God was dealing with me before I became consciously aware that He was real in my life. His first clear attempt was the day my gallery was raided in November of 1979. I knew without a doubt that the police were coming. It was God who informed me. Next, the Bible I found on the floor and the voice that spoke to my heart to take the Bible and read it. The next clear communication from God came when He spoke again and commanded I read the Bible like a book. These were the times that I surely know that God was making Himself clear to me. I remember these experiences as if they happened yesterday.

It was not that I thought that I was anyone special, but God was working through my circumstances. It was the hand of God that permitted various things to happen to me throughout my life and prevented others. I suppose if I had made the wrong decision at various points I would not have been able to see His hand working in my present situations.

I used to think it was all me. I used to think I was lucky. I didn't understand why, but many others suffered more than I did. I could see that fact through my life's experiences. It showed in my use of drugs and the various health problems I did not have. It appeared in the actual amount of jail time some received for breaking the same laws I did. It was revealed in the destructive attitudes and behaviors developed by others who were involved in the life to the same degrees I was exposed, but it wasn't because of me. Something else was at work. These are some of the hidden things that will be revealed at the end.

Once I got into reading the Bible I began to understand that the Spirit of God was moving constantly to open my mind to His reality. One night while I was reading the Bible I was in a state of depression. I felt useless and furthermore worthless. It was impressed upon me to count my blessings. I came up with three. I was not dead. I was not in jail and I was in good health. These blessings did not seem to be very important to me at the time, but they proved to be all I needed to change my life with the help of God.

The Bible tells a complete story. All of its parts fit together to reveal God's grand scheme of things. The story of God revealed in the Bible shattered my concepts of life and religion. All my knowledge of God was based on what I saw of religious people and the church experiences of my youth. What people said about God and what I saw of them who had something to say about God formed my perception of Him. After reading the Bible for myself I knew my perceptions of God were wrong. The people I heard and saw were all misrepresenting God on their best day. Nothing I experienced as a child in the Baptist tradition prepared me for this. The God of the Bible who identifies Himself did not resemble the God that was reflected to me as a child at all.

I believe in my heart that those of the faith had a true belief in Christ. Where they lacked is in their communication and understanding of what God promises to do for his people this side of heaven and what God fully expects from those called to the faith.

The God of the Bible is without fault and above question. He is a living God. He is a caring God. The God of the Bible works personally in everyone's life. He is not distant. He is right here right now battling against evil and unrighteousness better known to man as sin. His constant purpose and desire is to save people from their ignorance of Him.

I was bamboozled. Everything I had come to believe about life was a lie. The lie cut so deep into my heart that I realized there was nothing redeemable in what I did or in who I was. All the wickedness I learned about nations and people

164

was real, but what was not revealed was the ultimate judgment awaiting all doers of unrighteousness including myself. In the street you say what goes around comes around. The Bible says you reap what you sow and if you live by the sword you die by the sword.

One problem I had was brought to my attention. I was only looking at the faults I could see in others. I was blind to my own. I thought that everybody was supposed to see things my way. I didn't look too deeply at myself or truly entertain other perspectives. The Bible instructed in Matthew 7:5 "Cast the beam out of your own eye then you will see clearly how to remove the mote in your brother's eye.... "

Looking at myself I understood that nothing good would come out of the wrong I had done. Not only would nothing good come out of my deeds, nothing good would become of me. It was made clear that I was an enemy of God. The Word of God further revealed I was mentally corrupted, morally bankrupt and totally selfish.

Most of the basic knowledge I gathered from life and the books I read I found in the Bible. God Himself, if not the Bible, was becoming the source of all wisdom for me. Everyone else was plagiarizing the Bible. Information I found in the

Prophet and As a Man Thinketh was already written in the Bible long before these men were born.

Now that I was beginning to consciously work with God in my life He was allowing me to see myself clearly for the first time. I was beginning to understand what was really going on. Observed wrong did not grant me the right to do wrong. You do not overcome evil with evil; you overcome evil with good. Two wrongs do not make a right. God allowed me to reflect upon the notions I'd formed on my relationships, my family, my children and the world. He allowed me to see my faults and the consequences my decisions had on those closest to me. He allowed me to see how baseless my life had become and not only my life, but also the world in which I lived.

My postulation of God came from knowing myself. My self-knowledge provided a template for me to see and reflect God. Being a true criminal, I understood the lifestyle. There is a pecking order in the streets. The toughest kid on the block was on the highest level in the pecking order. You don't mess with this guy because he is the toughest kid on the block. The toughest had his act together. He could talk s*&#@ and back it up all the way. God was talking like He was the toughest kid on the block.

God announces Himself as the toughest there ever was and the toughest there ever will be. Throughout the Bible and especially in the latter chapters of the book of Job (38-41) God reveals Himself to Job and boasts of His greatness. He testifies to His splendor through His accomplishments in creation. One of the phrases expressed by God that captured my heart in the Bible is, I am the first and the last; before me there was none and after me there shall be none. Read any book of the Bible and see for yourself; God talks some stuff and promises to back it up. He talks like He means business. God essentially states that He is at the top of the pecking order in life. For further clarification He states that Job is the most righteous man in all the earth and that He was infinitely greater than Job. I was trusting He was all that He said He was and more. It was reassuring and a comfort to know this. I said to myself, I could go for this guy. Him and I are going to be all right.

As His image began to form in my understanding, conviction came. I knew I needed to change. Making that change was the most difficult task I had yet to face. The change could not be gradual. It had to be drastic. In my opinion I knew and understood all I needed about life and the world I lived in. Things were definitely black and white, but this was outside of and way beyond my frame of reference.

In my own understanding I was nobody in the eyes of White America. I was considered a bad guy from jump-street. I lived with no regrets. Because I lived like this, mainstream society would use this as an excuse to further justify dehumanizing me. I believed no one was going to give me a break. I bemoaned where would I fit if things were to change for me? Where was I going to go? What was I going to do? Coming out of a life of crime would be difficult enough as it is without having the annoyance of others looking over my shoulders. These concerns tormented me. That was my dilemma.

In the summer of 1980, I'm well into the Bible. By now I am talking to God regularly. I have running conversations with Him. I am discussing everything with Him, especially the problems I'm having trusting Him in the real world. Even though He talks back I'm not quite sure at this time if I'm out of my mind and just don't know it. My questions to Him distilled down to three issues. Who was going to pay my rent, buy my food and put clothes on my back if I followed Christ? God responds and says quit or die. My insides are in turmoil.

I know that I have to change the way I am living. I have to go all the way with God. God was giving me an out, but He hadn't definitively revealed Himself to me in the material world. I just knew him as the spiritual or almighty God revealed through the Bible. I wasn't sure God was running things here and now. I needed to be sure. I had to get this God stuff right, no mistakes. I had gotten to the point where I believed if I didn't quit hustling, I was going to die. That's when the written Word or I say Logos Word began to present itself to me as real in my practical life. God spoke specifically to me and confirmed it in the written words of the Bible. God spoke Matthew 6:33 into my spirit; seek ye first the kingdom of God and His righteousness and all these things will be added.

Verse 33 of the book of Matthew is the action statement arising from the examples and explanations given by Jesus starting in verse 25. These passages teach that the body and life itself is more real and important to God than our material needs. Christ explains Himself from His worldview or life perspective. He uses birds, which are provided for in life by God. The point made is if God takes care of living creatures of lesser importance than humans He would of course provide for us.

He next expresses the beauty of plant life. He uses lilies in a field as an analogy and compares their splendor with the splendor of Solomon. After reading the account of Solomon's life and reign as the 3$^{rd}$ king of Israel in the Old Testament it is revealed that Solomon was the greatest man of his time. He was the greatest in wisdom and the greatest in material splendor. None in his day could compare with him and the account in the Bible declares that after him none will ever compare or be greater. With all that said, God states plainly that the lilies and the grass are nothing, yet He beautifies them. If He is willing to beautify creations of no eternal value how much more would He beautifully array those who had faith in Him. Matters of the world or self-conscience have no bearing on what God can and will do for the faithful.

This meant that God would meet my every need. It made no difference that I was a Black Man in a racially conscious nation. It did not make a difference that I was a soon to be ex-criminal without social assets. All that mattered was my belief that God is whom He says He is and that He would do what He said He would do. If I could do that I would have nothing to worry about.

If God is the toughest being in existence He could back up all those big words expressed in Matthew chapter 6. That is one of the reasons I believe the institutional church, as I knew it was misrepresenting God on its best day. No one I ever knew preached a message as simply and clearly as expressed in Matthew chapter 6. The message, believe in God and do things the way He says and everything, I mean everything you will need in life will be provided for you by God. Why? I took the passage literally. God was really involved in every aspect of my life and He really cared about me above all else. This was a lesson I could test in the here and now to know if God was here and now, proving that He was real to me.

I begin to read the Bible through for the second time. I always had a philosophy in hustling to never go to jail for killing anybody and you don't die in the streets. Just don't die out here. According to my thinking you only go to jail for making money. As long as you're making money, it's ok to go to jail. If you're not making money, no way, that's plain stupid. God let me know in my heart that I was going to die. I can't die out here. It's time for me to get out.

I begin to mentally prepare myself to quit the life I knew. It's not an easy thing to step out of the life. Not because of outward pressures, more so because it's all I know. I had become what I did. People depended on me. I was a ringleader. I was a money maker. In fact, I paid peoples' rent and fed peoples' faces. If I were to leave, their quality of life would suffer. That became an issue and a question in my mind. In truth, I really cared about the people I was around. I had to work that out in my mind. There was a lot of stuff I would need to face if I was going to make this transition. It was almost like I was losing my mind along with my heart. Actually I was, but the word of God says in Matthew 10:39, He who loses his life for Christ's sake shall find it and he who finds his life shall lose it.

I'm coming toward the end of 1980 and I am totally convinced I must quit, it's just a matter of time. I needed to get ready.

It is common knowledge that many men cheat or have cheated on their women. It is also common knowledge that the other woman is more often than not aware the man is cheating. Living for the moment or for self-gratification is the underlying rationalization for this behavior. If I were having too much difficulty in my primary relationship I would seek comfort and companionship in the affections of another woman. I was justified because any problems encountered were the woman's fault and I assuredly did not deserve the grief she was giving me.

In the summer of 1979 I was in such a situation with Diane. That summer I met and began a relationship with Regina Webb. As my problems with Diane increased I thought things would be better for me with Regina. I was wrong. I left Diane and moved in with Regina. After a few months I abandoned Regina and returned to Diane. To complicate matters more Regina was pregnant. In September of 1980 my son Walter III was born.

My returning to a woman was a first for me and it was a humbling experience. I had never felt responsible for a woman in that way before. I could see that I was a major contributor to the problems we were facing. I had done her wrong. I felt a need to make up for my mistakes. I wanted to try to do better if I was given the chance.

Regina had an apartment on 238th and Bailey Ave. in the Bronx where I met Mario Disdiel a neighbor from next door. Mario was a Cuban and had extensive experience in incense manufacturing. Incense was a rage in the 60's and 70's as the U.S. drug culture came to maturity. During that period Mario made a lot of money in that business. At the time I met him he was interested in going back into the business, but he didn't have the start up capital.

To cover my bases I felt it was necessary to develop an alternative means of support for myself once I quit selling drugs. I reached out to Mario. He assured me that he could restart a decent incense operation with a couple of thousand dollars. I put up the cash. Along with that investment I purchased two more sedans to lease as gypsy cabs. I went on shopping sprees buying any and everything I thought that I would need. I bought clothing, footwear, electronics and anything else of value. I paid the rent on my apartment for a year. I did all of this to prepare for what I thought was to come.

I was trying to prepare myself for what I perceived God to be doing in my life. I knew the handwriting was on the wall. Do you know that phrase originates in the Bible? I knew I was going to quit hustling and I was preparing for the inevitable.

After I was sure it was God, I began to share with Buster and others I was in deep with that I was about to quit. No one believed me. I tried to encourage them to follow me. No one took me up on it. I set the date. The New Year seemed to be the ideal time. I'm saying to myself I'm going to walk away on January 1st, 1981. January 1st came…I didn't quit. I missed my deadline.

"OK God, Ok. February 1st, I'll quit."

February first comes. I missed again. I couldn't quit. I'd had enough. If I was going to do this then I had to do it. I set my mind and the next date for me to quit for March 1, 1981. February 28th came. I left alone. I went home from my spot for the last time. I took $5,000.00 in cash and all the other goods I had squirreled away. March 1, 1981 I was no longer a criminal. I had begun to identify myself as a man of God.

The
University of the State of New York
Education Department

Be it known that

WALTER WILSON

*having satisfactorily completed the comprehensive examination requirements*
*prescribed by the Commissioner of Education*
*is thereby entitled to this*

## High School Equivalency Diploma

**In Witness Whereof** *the Regents issue this diploma*
*under seal of the University at Albany in the 1973 series*

*President of the University*
*and Commissioner of Education*

1ˢᵗ  G.E.D.

THE UNIVERSITY OF THE STATE OF NEW YORK
THE STATE EDUCATION DEPARTMENT
HIGH SCHOOL EQUIVALENCY TESTING PROGRAM
ALBANY, NEW YORK 12224

## TRANSCRIPT OF SCORES

TESTS OF GENERAL EDUCATIONAL DEVELOPMENT

of the

AMERICAN COUNCIL ON EDUCATION

Walter Wilson
2027 7th Avenue
New York, New York 10027

Testing Date: 12/6/72
028-3100

A high school equivalency diploma is issued by the New York State Education Department to any eligible candidate who obtains **both** a score of 35 or more on each of the Tests of General Educational Development **and** a total standard score of 225 or more for all five of the tests.

| Test No. | Name of Test |
|---|---|
| 1 | Correctness and Effectiveness of Expression |
| 2 | Interpretation of Reading Materials in the Social Studies |
| 3 | Interpretation of Reading Materials in the Natural Sciences |
| 4 | Interpretation of Literary Materials |
| 5 | General Mathematical Ability |

Your scores for each of the five most recently taken tests are listed below, to the right of each test number and test form. Your total score is listed under the individual scores.

| | | | Test No. | Test Form | Score |
|---|---|---|---|---|---|
| WILSON | WALTER | 028 3100 | 1 | AA | 54 |
| | | | 2 | AA | 59 |
| | | | 3 | AA | 56 |
| | | | 4 | AA | 59 |
| | | | 5 | AA | 58 |
| | | | | | 286 |

☐ Scores satisfactory, diploma issued.

☐ Scores satisfactory, diploma not issued. When you become fully eligible for the diploma, you should write this office requesting it.

☑ Scores not satisfactory, diploma not issued. Attach this score report to your application when you apply for retesting. Read the reverse side of this form. We have examined both your scores listed above and your scores on these circled test forms:

H    J    K    L    EE    FF    GG    AA    BB    SA    SB    SC

DRT 617 (7-72-50,000)
36972

**Test score**

177

Be it known that

WALTER WILSON

*having satisfactorily completed the requirements prescribed by the Commissioner of Education is thereby entitled to this*

## High School Equivalency Diploma

**In Witness Whereof** *the Regents issue this diploma under seal of the University at Albany in the 197 4 series*

*Gerald B. Reggivirt*
*President of the University*
*and Commissioner of Education*

178

**2<sup>nd</sup> G.E.D.**

THE UNIVERSITY OF THE STATE OF NEW YORK
THE STATE EDUCATION DEPARTMENT
HIGH SCHOOL EQUIVALENCY TESTING PROGRAM
ALBANY, NEW YORK 12224

TRANSCRIPT OF SCORES

TESTS OF GENERAL EDUCATIONAL DEVELOPMENT
of the
AMERICAN COUNCIL ON EDUCATION

•

Walter Wilson
237 W. 131st Street
NY, NY  10027

Testing Date: 11/21/73
028-8134

•

A high school equivalency diploma is issued by the New York State Education Department to any eligible candidate who obtains **both** a score of 35 or more on each of the Tests of General Educational Development **and** a total standard score of 225 or more for all five of the tests.

| Test No. | Name of Test |
|---|---|
| 1 | Correctness and Effectiveness of Expression |
| 2 | Interpretation of Reading Materials in the Social Studies |
| 3 | Interpretation of Reading Materials in the Natural Sciences |
| 4 | Interpretation of Literary Materials |
| 5 | General Mathematical Ability |

Your scores for each of the five most recently taken tests are listed below, to the right of each test number and test form. Your total score is listed under the individual scores.

| | Test No. | Form | Score |
|---|---|---|---|

☑ Scores satisfactory,
diploma issued

028  8134   Test 1  HH  55
2  66
3  59
4  63
5  55
Total  298

☐ Scores satisfactory, diploma not issued. When you become fully eligible for the diploma, you should write this office requesting it.

☐ Scores not satisfactory, diploma not issued. Attach this score report to your application when you apply for retesting. Read the reverse side of this form. We have examined both your scores listed above and your scores on these circled test forms.

H    J    K    L    EE    FF    GG    AA    BB    SA    SB    SC

DET 611 (7-72-50,000)
36972

**Test score**

179

Top left- My daughter Tesha
Top right- Walter and Rose Bayne, Lamar's        mother
Bottom left- Tesha and her sister Lacresia
Bottom right- My son Lamar and his cousin        Robin

Top- Mother and son

Bottom- Stanley "Jellybean" Green

181

Top- Hangin' on the Avenue        Middle- Fellas on 126 <sup>th</sup> Street

Bottom- Diane and Yvette

182

RA-MEL

Prison photos

Bottom- Mark and Keith, faking it

183

Top- Myrna                    Bottom- Diane

Top- Walter, L.A., and Keith

Bottom- Larenzo Anderson, a.k.a. L.A.

185

Top- Mark "Stock-O-Lick" Stewart with Vicki

Bottom- Buster

Top- Diane and I　　　Middle- At the top of my game
Bottom- Approaching the end

187

Top- Diane, Cheryl and Regina (Walter III's          mother) in the park

Bottom- Out of the life raising my son, Walter III

188

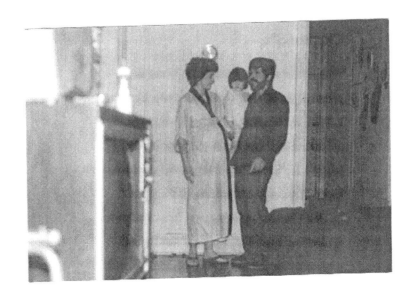

Top- Mario Disdiel with family        Bottom- my new enterprise

## Chapter Six

With all I had been through I still was not
prepared for all God was about to do. On March
1, 1981 not much had changed in me. The big
difference was that I was no longer headed
towards 8 <sup>th</sup> Ave. to sell drugs and commune with
known criminals and cohorts of the street.
Instead I headed uptown in the Bronx to learn
the trade of manufacturing and distributing
incense under the tutelage of Mario Disdiel. The
real difference was to learn how to see my life
and the world through the eyes of God and yield
to that understanding.

I spoke to God regularly as I was learning and
adjusting to my new way of life. I had this
conversational relationship with God, but I never
kneeled down when I would pray. A man doesn't
bow to anyone and other presumptions of my past
still lingered in my heart. The process of internal
change was just beginning. Who knew?

Mario did know the incense business, but things
had changed since he was last involved. Many of
his suppliers were no longer around. After a little
hunting we located a chemical dealer in the
South Bronx who knew Mario and was still in
business. Through him we were able to purchase

the incense oils and DPL to create our fragrances. We purchased our punk sticks from wholesalers in downtown Manhattan along with other essentials needed to package and label our product. Next we had to identify a location where we could manufacture and store our supplies.

I realized immediately that all I knew about selling drugs was directly applicable to the practice of selling incense. Yet two problems arose that neither Mario nor I anticipated. One was the saturated incense market and the other, a major decrease in the use of incense by the consumer. Every store we entered had several brands of incense hanging unsold in their stores. We were not able to establish our hoped distribution network. We ended up stuck with several thousand dollars worth of merchandise and no way to move it.

At the same time I was trying to identify people who would be willing to lease my cars to use as gypsy cabs. Finding honest and dependable people is very difficult. Things refused to work out. Over a three-month period all three of my vehicles were totaled leaving me without a means of support. Mario in response to my disappointment suggested that we sell the incense ourselves. The area we chose was

Fordham Road in the Bronx. It was also clear that we should end our partnership and go our separate ways.

I would work the street on at my location off Webster Ave. and Fordham Road Thursday, Friday and Saturday when most people were out shopping. On Monday I would shop for supplies, Tuesday I would dip my incense and Wednesday I would package my product. My income dropped from 3 to 5 thousand dollars a day to maybe $200.00 a week.

To increase my income I tried to encourage a few of the fellows hanging around my neighborhood to sell incense on various corners in the Bronx. Soon I had two young men working. One worked 170 th and the Grand concourse and the other worked Tremont Ave. Neither gentleman worked out. I tightened my belt and continued. A little money was better than no money at all.

When working on Fordham I kept my Bible on the table, which I continued to read, but I also read other religious literature. I read material on the Ansaru Allah community, the Hebrew Israelites, the Black Muslims, and the Jehovah witnesses. I read information on the eastern religions including Hinduism and Budism. I read the Autobiography of a Yogi, by Paramahansa

Yogananda. All of them professed a view divergent from Christianity. The information learned helped broaden my spiritual understanding. It also helped me understand people of other religious beliefs.

Though I considered myself a Christian, I did not attend any religious services, associate myself with any or other professing Christians. I was searching and didn't want any unnecessary distractions. Others tended to be dogmatic in their beliefs.

One cold day in late 1981 I saw Myrna, my old girlfriend shopping on Fordham Road. When I saw her my first sense was one of embarrassment followed by shame. I didn't want her to see me. After spotting me she approached and asked me to stop by her house at the end of my day because she wanted to talk to me.

I had deliberately dropped out of sight after I stopped hustling. I just disappeared and quit frequenting all of my old hangouts. I guess those who were closest to me had some questions around what happened. Myrna was a hustler through and through. When I arrived at her house she had a proposition for me. At the time she was stashing and moving quinine from her home. She wanted me to consider partnering with her to move heroine. She would handle the quinine and I would handle street distribution of the drugs.

It was a good deal. Moving quinine is as lucrative as moving heroine. Quinine is a necessary ingredient in cutting dope. If she could guarantee the ingredients to cut drugs major distributors would come knocking at our door. This was a guaranteed moneymaker. I was tempted.

I was on a low. The cars were gone and I was stuck on Fordham Road selling incense making a couple of hundred dollars a week if that much. Maybe this was what I was supposed to do. I was reluctant but interested. She sensed my hesitation and gave me a small package to sell. If I liked it I could decide.

The next day I took the package and I found myself on 8th Ave. I did not return to the spot because I was not trying to draw attention to myself. My first realization was that I had no desire to be on the streets selling drugs. I was so uncomfortable. I also had difficulty expressing my intentions to various fiends whom I remembered. Finally after giving away several samples the testers began to return and express their opinion as to the quality of the drugs. The product was excellent. Instead of excitement I

194

was overcome with fear. It was clear to me that I was no longer suited for a life of crime. God had clearly spoken. I walked 127th Street towards St. Nicolas Ave. dropped the remaining heroine in a sewer caught the train and went home. I didn't bother to contact Myrna again. She would be able to deduce my decision from my actions.

When I walked away from the spot the only thing I quit was crime, but that was not enough. God was not finished with me. On the contrary He was just beginning. When I left I still sniffed cocaine, smoked reefer, cigarettes and drank alcohol. These were habits I could no longer afford. I had to stop using cocaine soon. The amount I ingested dropped dramatically once I left the streets. I was down to spending about $50.00 a week on the weekends. After a couple of months I was able to stop altogether. Next I focused on cigarette smoking and drinking. I was reluctant to give up marijuana. After two years I was completely pollutant free. I even gave up fornication. I married Diane in June of 1982.

Diane and I lived at 1347 Morris Ave. in the Bronx. In late 1981 the building Diane and I lived in was abandoned by the landlord and condemned. That winter with no heat, we froze. Earlier in the year our apartment had been burglarized three times in less than a three-week period. Everything I tried to put together to sustain me in my new life was gone. I was left with nothing. Pressure was building. Diane was working, but we could not keep it together. I was determined not to give up. I guess I could have begun to look for a job, but I did not believe that was what I was supposed to do. In part it was because I wanted more for myself than what I thought I could command working; in part I still didn't believe I would get a fair shake from society.

With all hope gone at 1347 Diane and I decided to move in with her mother. I dreaded the move. Her mother still lived in the St. Nicholas Houses. If I returned I would be accessible and available for all eyes to see. I wasn't comfortable with my circumstances and I didn't want anyone to see me in my present state.

My fears quickly caught up with me after moving in. For the most part I kept to myself and minded my own business. Most people who knew me dared not question me. When a few did I would say I am into God and keep it moving.

One day a young man who knew me better than most singled me out. He was still in the game. Being bold he laughed at me out loud in the company of his friends as I was passing by. At the same time he called my name. Hey Walt, what's up? I hear you are into this God thing. Look at you. You are not doing so good, ha? A rage welled up in me immediately. I wanted to slap him on the spot. I was prepared to go the rest of the way if necessary. Instead I kept walking.

I did not know what to do with my rage. As I continued walking I asked God what to do. I wanted to believe I could return to crime to protect myself from such insults, but I knew that couldn't be the answer.

God spoke to my heart and said, Walter, What makes you a man, the God in your heart or the money in your pocket? I knew what money in my pocket would do for me, but I wasn't sure what God would do for me in the real world. I decided to give God a chance. At that point as I was walking down the street I began to cry. I was crying big boo hoo tears. I couldn't believe it. Here I was a grown man crying. I hadn't shed a tear since I was twelve years old. In all those years I had forgotten how to cry.

By the time I had gotten to Diane's mother's house my nose was running and everything. When I finished crying my rage was gone. It was a good feeling. Crying before God had brought about a release that freed me from my anger. I surrendered to and made a promise to God. As a criminal I had hard hustled and served the devil from 17 to 30, a total of thirteen years. I told God that I would serve Him for thirteen years. If He in those thirteen years could do me better than the devil then I would serve Him for the rest of my life. I didn't know it then, but God beat the devil in six.

This experience with God brought me to a new level of humility. In all my talking with God I could never bring myself to kneel before Him. As I continued my relationship with God I found myself on my knees more often as I spoke to Him, especially in the mornings and evenings as I began and ended my days.

I continued to sell incense while living in the St. Nick, but things were becoming more difficult for me. At first it was easy to get a peddlers license, but the policy changed and the issued licenses were reserved for veterans. Without a license I would not be able to continue to sell on the streets. From time to time the city would crack down on street peddlers. When this would happen the police would harass and ticket unlicensed persons caught peddling merchandise on the street. I wasn't making enough money to go through this aggravation so I quit.

I needed to find something to get into. I couldn't accomplish anything doing nothing. My old contacts were of no use to me in my new life. Since God had come into my life I hadn't developed any new relationships. My focus was on deliverance, healing and reconciliation. I was not sure how to present myself to people due to my criminal history and previous lifestyle; neither did I have an idea of where I could go to present myself, but I knew I was changed. I believed if I were given a chance others would be able to see for themselves that I was capable and of value. I decided to volunteer. I might not be able to find work with a salary due to my past, but I was sure there was someone who would allow me to work for free. After that it would be up to me.

I hit the streets. Reading flyers and other handouts I learned about and began attending community meetings. My practice was to arrive early and stay late. This allowed me to learn as much as I could about the goings on. I met some of Harlem's greatest making my rounds. Two of note was Kofi Brown and Ed "Pork Chop" Davis, the last of the "step ladder preachers." Under their tutelage I learned the art and history of community activism. Eventually I became intimately involved with the Saint Nicholas Houses Tenants Association. The association was under the leadership of Ms Willie Mae Lewis the president and her vice president Ms Mack. This was my entrée into Harlem politics.

Arriving early I started helping them set up for their monthly meetings. Then I stayed after the meetings to help breakdown and clean the room. I made myself available for them to use if needed. Every opportunity that presented itself to me, I was there and took advantage of it. I mean whatever they needed if it was within my ability I offered myself. After a couple of months I was attending some meetings on behalf of the association and reporting to the president and vice president. I was grateful to them and to God for the trust they extended to me.

My association with Ms Lewis and Ms Mack validated me as a changed person. New doors began to open to learn new things and develop other relationships. I was becoming more involved with the Harlem community at large. I also became more involved with the tenants of the development and residents of the community at large. I was no stranger to Ms Lewis or Ms

Mack. Both were long standing residents of the projects. They knew exactly who I was. Other members of the association also knew.

Ms Mary, a resident of my mother's building approached me one day and reported her observations of me. She said Walter you were a bad boy. Playing ignorant I responded, why do you say that Ms Mary? She then recounted a time she saw me rob the supermarket on 8$^{th}$ Ave. in broad daylight for all to see. I knew exactly what she was talking about. She further stated that from that time on she had nothing good to say about me and kept as much distance from me as she could. But now she saw a change in me and was comfortable around me, seeing how I was being so helpful to others.

I learned through conversations many of the tenants could not understand most of the policies and regulations the Housing Authority and other government agencies would implement. Every change brought on a new flurry of concern. It was worse for the elderly. They were bombarded with literature from Medicare, Social Security, tax filings and more. The more policies changed, the more confused and helpless they became. I found myself assisting as many as I could.

It was a blessing to me to be able to help so many. I began to read their mail and advise them accordingly. I wrote letters, escorted them to the hospital and clinic, I took them shopping, to the bank, to the rent office and assisted some with their budget. Sometimes they would give me a few dollars and other times just their gratitude. Both helped and I was thankful. What a difference God was making.

With the Tenants Association as my nucleus I continued to attend other meetings. A fledgling organization was hosting meetings in the Adam Clayton Powell State Office Building on 125th Street. It existed under the name M.O.R.E., Motivational Organization Researching in Economics. They were interested in finding and developing ways they could invest to create wealth. I was present at their next regularly scheduled meeting.

The night I attended they were soliciting oral investment proposals from attendees that would be of interest to the group. I took the opportunity to speak to the group. They were not drawn to my suggestion, but my presentation caught the attention of Joseph Holland who was attending the meeting.

After the meeting he introduced himself and invited me to attend a Thursday night bible study he hosted in a brownstone on 148th Street in Harlem. The next Thursday I was there. I was impressed. The room was full of young Black people discussing passages of the Bible. Everyone seemed so well versed. After the bible study I hung around to get more information. As I conversed with a number of attendees all my inquiries were directed towards two young gentlemen, Joseph Holland, who invited me to the study and James O'Neal. This was what I was praying for.

As the crowd thinned I spoke to both Joe and James. They were very open and forth coming. I knew I was entering a new learning curve. For one it was the first time I heard the word vision used as an objective. These two men were recent graduates of Harvard University School of Law. During their studies they founded a Christian organization and called it Harlem's Ark of Freedom (HARK). Their vision for the organization was to utilize the gifts and abilities they and other Christian graduates of Harvard had available to them to uplift the residents of the Harlem community through the knowledge of Jesus Christ.

While in school they had recruited others who were willing to labor to make their vision a reality. James and Joe had already completed their studies and graduated. They arrived in part to lay the foundation for the other core members who were still in school, but soon to be graduating. I eventually met and was befriended by them all. Each was equally committed to their professed cause. These young accomplished Blacks were willing to sacrifice their earned opportunities to give back to improve the quality of the lives of those less fortunate than themselves. Any one of them qualified to receive work with upper 5 figure salaries in a place of their choosing.

The members of this elite group were comprised of Leslie Walker, Jacqueline Patton, Mary Ann Royal and Dennis Henderson to name a few.

Their background and acculturation was diametrically opposed to mine, but at the core of our beings wed the same desire. I was determined to be involved. Every aspect resonated with me from within. What I brought to the table was the testimony of what God was doing in my life, my being a native Harlemite with a working knowledge of the community and

I was game for everything. I was fully accepted as a charter member of HARK.

My spiritual eyes were opening. God was developing new relationships and opportunities for me in the real world. Yes, God is a spiritual being, but he was proving to me that He alone is in charge of and ultimately in total control of the physical realm. Within the fellowship of HARK my coarser tendencies were being refined. I was being groomed. I began to develop by leaps and bounds, becoming more comfortable with God and myself with each God guided experience.

It was with HARK I began to attend church services consistently. It was with HARK I formally confessed Jesus Christ as my Lord and Savior at an altar. It was in HARK I attended my first deliverance service and discovered a spirit of violence in me. At that same service I was baptized in the Holy Spirit. It was in HARK I reconsidered the institutional church as a relative institution for the well being of the broader African American community.

During my fellowship with HARK the last vestiges of my outward sinful behavior was vanquished. I stopped smoking marijuana. The real battles took place more in the spiritual and mental arenas. The perspective from which I processed information began to change. I began to yield to the principle truths of God.

Spiritually I had to unlearn all I thought I knew and learn how to think Godly. Feelings emanated from my heart that led to thoughts, thoughts led to behaviors, behaviors to habits and habits back to my heart. This was a vicious cycle that needed to be broken. My own thought process tormented me. The factors I rested within this cycle were corrupted. In my difficulty God drew my attention to Jude 8. I had to address myself on the thought level. What I thought ultimately led to my emotional distress. I was having such a hard time with myself because I was trying to change my behavior. The new realization was that to fight and win all that was necessary was to rebuke my own thoughts and trust God to do the rest.

I walked around for days rebuking the thoughts, ideas and conclusions that pervaded my mind. I prayed earnestly for my ultimate victory. At the heart of my distress lay fear. I was afraid of being taken advantage of. I wasn't into exposing my feelings not to mention letting someone hurt them if I could help it. I wanted to be regarded in life. Jacqueline Patton gave me some advice in those days that opened my eyes. She told me that

I could not win every battle. To be effective I would have to learn how to pick and choose my battles. I used to practice that truth once upon a time, but I wasn't applying it in my conversion.

The Bible speaks of love as the most powerful behavior a person can demonstrate. In my mind love was interpreted as kindness and kindness was equated with weakness. How did one protect their heart from those who would take advantage of them? Still I had to convince myself God was right. I had to replace fear with love. I had to learn how to practice the art of love. I had to see kindness as strength and recognize those who abused kindness as weak; a complete reversal of ideas. The removal of that linchpin released me from my bondage. My deliverance appeared gradually and subtly. One day I realized my mind was at rest. I didn't have any desire to get high. I wasn't lusting for sex neither did I have any vengeful thoughts. My heart was clear and I was thankful.

I encountered many new experiences during this period in my walk of faith. Many shadows hovered over my life that were unbeknownst to me, yet accepted as reality. During my days of crime many dark doors were opened. I terrorized many. At some point I robbed an older woman who ran a numbers operation out of her home. Under the street code (usually unspoken) if you didn't have the strength to keep what you had, you don't deserve to have it. I stormed into her place like death on two feet. I accomplished the perfect effect and escaped with the day's receipts.

From time to time over the years I would see this older woman and she would cringe in fear at my appearance. One day in 1983 I was in prayer walking up 8th Ave. As I saw the woman I was overcome with remorse. I was told to approach her, apologize and ask for her forgiveness. Boy that was a challenge. I slowed my pace, took a deep breath and turned towards the woman. A look of terror seized her face. I quickly found some words of comfort and assurance to offer her. I told her I was sorry for what I did. I told her I would never do anything like that again and I asked her to forgive me.

As the words spilled from my mouth it became clear that a miracle was taking place. The sigh of relief the woman expressed lifted a burden I did not know I carried. Afterward I felt a weight lifted off of me. My gait was lighter and I possessed more freedom to express myself than ever before in life. This and more was going on in my life as I became more enveloped in the agendas of HARK.

Things weren't improving between Diane and me. We never really addressed what was going on. We just drifted apart. Any attempts on my part to address the matter were met with silence. I was pushing hard to address what I believed God was doing in my life. I was jobless, but I still believed it was not in my best interest to look for a job. My wife did not agree and seemed not to appreciate all that was happening within and around me.

Between 1983 and 1984 I became accustomed to being broke. The passage that reads, My God shall provide your needs according to His riches in glory in Christ Jesus, was made real to me. God never states that He will provide your wants only your needs. That understanding was essential to my weathering this financial storm.

I had to learn how to hold on to a dollar and make due with what I didn't have. God proved Himself to be my provider while delivering me from material assumptions I assumed over my life. There was not one day I went without food to eat, clean clothes to wear or a roof over my head with a decent place to sleep.

It was always a challenge to keep my focus on what was important. Every so often something would come up. I was riding down in the elevator one day with a group of others. Ricky, my brother-in-law was on the elevator with me. He made a comment at that time poking fun at my present circumstances. I wasn't personally offended as in times past. I did not have the urge to hurt in return though the comment was made at my expense. In response I stated that things had been financially better in the past, but I am making long range plans now. Once I pass this station I will never have need to return. I realized I had grown.

Though I was broke I felt good about myself. I felt good about what I was doing about the quality and conditions of my life. I believed I was on the right course.

By 1984 my marriage was in trouble. Our relationship had changed. I felt Diane was being unfair. It seemed she was punishing me because of my infidelity. I had lost her trust and her confidence. I believed I had to regain her trust. I took responsibility for the failure of our marriage. With the help of God, amends would be made. I began to search my heart in earnest to get to the root of my problem in my relating to women in general and Diane specifically. I even seriously thought about finding a job.

In April of that year I was forced to leave my wife. I was murderously angry. I had no idea of what was going on. I had changed so dramatically towards what I thought to be the better. Was this my return on trying to do right? I couldn't believe Diane didn't want me around. The way I saw it I was a much better person and I was making a courageous effort to get even better. I asked myself how she couldn't see and appreciate what was going on. Underneath, my anger towards her raged. I needed to find a neutral place to consider what was going on and God presented HARK. James O'Neal and Joseph Holland were there when I needed God most.

I had three problems: 1) my anger at my wife Diane. 2) If I left my marriage I had no place to go, and 3) what was God up to? The answers provided for the first two problems settled the question of the third. The first evening I kept them up all night. That sat and ministered to my hurts. We concluded it was best for me to stay away for a while. I agreed. I was in no condition to be alone or in an unhealthy environment. After four days under the prayerful eyes of Joe and

James, God had done a work and my decision was made.

I had to move back in with my mother. The idea of a grown man living with his mother and her providing for him didn't agree with my understanding of things, but I had to swallow my pride. As for my marriage I had to accept the wishes of my wife and leave. I couldn't make her want me and if I tried, it wouldn't work. God's question to me in that situation was why was I so enraged? Coming to an understanding of my emotional response and growing beyond that limitation was God's challenge to me. That was the most important issue at hand.

Confronting my anger with my wife brought deeper revelations. No wife meant, no sex. For the first time in 20 years I wouldn't have a woman in my life. If I had sex I would be an adulterer. Not only would I be in sin if I had sex, I would be leading a woman into sin with me. I was bound. I had become a prisoner of my knowledge of God. To heighten the stakes God informed me, no separation and no divorce. The only way I saw out and to please God was sexual abstinence. I had no desire to live without sex. The question became, did I need to have sex and could I do without it?

Addressing my sexual desires was a major undertaking. The battle was on. The battle was fought physically, mentally and spiritually. The fact that I liked sex didn't help at all. I refused to engage in intercourse. If I couldn't do right I wouldn't involve anyone else in doing wrong. After two years I had reached my goal.

My ordeal had brought to the forefront, the truth that spirits are real. Dark spirits are real. I knew two spirits had befriended me during my sinful past, unbeknownst to me at the time. One was a spirit of violence the other a spirit of lust.

By nature I was not a violent man. During my early days in the streets I went through a transformation and learned to employ violence as a means to an end. I believe I introduced the spirit of violence into my life when I seriously hurt Ron in prison because he had hurt me. I had a vengeful spirit if you will. If hurt emotionally or otherwise, or truly threatened, the consideration of crippling force became a reasonable option. Not as an idea, but as a course of action. Something changed within me that day. I didn't know what it was then, but I could sense it. After that I didn't have any more problems with other inmates.

My anger at Diane erupted from that spirit. What was wrong with her? She hurt me. She used me. She took advantage of me. I wanted revenge. She rejected me. I wanted her to hurt too.

The other spirit was one of lust. After my experience of rejection at 15 I determined to get me a girl. Mind you, I didn't know what to do with one, but I knew I had to get one. I surely wasn't prepared to befriend, love or provide for one. That left the most physical option available, sex. If you have a girl you have to have sex. I believe that level of ignorance opened the door for a spirit of lust. Looking back I realized that I had always had a girlfriend from that time on even during my times in prison.

In April of 1984 I moved back into 240 with my mother. My returning to my mother's home at the time I did was a blessing. I left a young man destined for trouble; a burden on my mother's heart. I returned a servant son determined to work out our time together. When I left Dorothy was my mother. When I returned I saw her for the first time as a woman. No doubt she always loved me, but this time we became friends.

At one point I asked her why she allowed me back into her home. When I left I was a crook and remained so. She told me that I was not a crook. She said I stole because I didn't have. When you have, you don't steal, you give. I didn't realize that about myself until she said it.

About three years into my conversion I got word that another crew had engaged a turf war for control of the building my old crew worked out of. Larenzo Anderson (L.A.) was killed. Buster was shot and left for dead and Marc Stewart eventually received life in prison. I knew that if I were still in the game I would have been in the center of that dispute. I know it would have been me they moved on first or maybe I would have made the first move. More importantly I know it was God who spared me from that appointment with death. Quit or die was the word I received from God just three years earlier.

The other crew worked 8th Ave. After I quit I encountered them on Fordham Road while selling incense. They were three deep as they exited the car. They double-parked in front of the pizza shop where I peddled. I didn't want them to see me at the time. They saw me and grinned. It was more like a snicker. They approached me as if to say look at us. They bought a few dollars worth of incense told me to keep the change and walked away. Two weeks later they returned and I was still there peddling away. This time they didn't even bother to come over.

Whatever actually happened during the period of the shootings I don't know? What I do know is God let them know I was no longer involved the day they saw me peddling incense on Fordham Road in the Bronx.

In July I got my first job since I was 19 or 20 years old. Ms Lewis the tenant association president had secured for me a summer job as a youth counselor paying $11.00 an hour. That was good money. It had taken four years for me to finally land a job.

I was living practically on nothing. My only pastime was the movies. I didn't spend money on anything else. I had nothing to do with the extra money, but save. It was an alright job. I liked working with the children and they liked me. By the end of that enjoyable summer I had saved over $2,000.00.

I wrestled with all of the insights I gained working with the tenants association, fellowshipping with HARK and living at home with my mother. As my physical and the mental torment came to an end I began to see what God was able to do with one who was willing to surrender to Him.

It is amazing how violently I resisted God. My human understanding led me to believe that I must avoid all the things I truly feared at all costs. God on the other hand confronts you with those fears and bids you to overcome them with His help. He promises to be there with you, but He looks to you to employ the knowledge of the faith He has provided as tools to conquer your doubts and fears.

The things I feared most had overcome me in the past. The person that developed in reaction to my fears was who I thought I was. I was not and I was wrong. God had led me to this place that I might confront them in His presence. Taking courage derived from God's promises I confronted them. Once honestly confronted the fear was replaced with a peace that was followed by a joy. My fears of being ridiculed and being less than a man melted away. The benefits received were spiritually provided and internally edifying. The experience was mind-boggling. I was becoming me, being comfortable with me and really getting to know me for the first time in my life.

I was ready to try making it on my own. I moved out of my mother's and into HARK's community residence on 137th Street off 8th Avenue. HARK leased an entire brownstone, which served as its living quarters and meeting place. The women occupied the first and second floors, while the men occupied the upper floors. The basement was used as the general meeting area.

To nurture interest for our causes HARK sponsored Harlem tours. Visitors to Harlem and other interested parties were escorted throughout the community. I proved to have an intimate knowledge of Harlem's history and its current affairs. What I didn't know I learned. Our charges were usually Christians from neighboring areas. On one such tour, I believe sponsored by Ramapo College in New Jersey, I met and was befriended by Mrs. Sandy Van Dyk a white woman from Franklin Lakes, N.J.

Most white people, after our initial meeting, would choose to keep their distance. Some middle class Blacks do the same. In one sense I view life from a non-traditional perspective. On the other hand I bring a lot to the table and have a lot to offer. My non-traditional perspective and criminal past is enough to frighten most from looking into what I have to offer. Sometimes I think that they are afraid that something I have might rub off on them. I anticipated that response from her. She proved to be different. She took every available opportunity to be in my presence. I did not know what to make of her. Now it was my turn to keep my distance. She persisted.

At the end of the tour as the group was about to depart she handed me a note and $60.00. The note read here is some money to buy these three books for you to read. I believe they will be of interest to you. Here is my phone number. Call me. I would like for you to take a tour of my neighborhood.

I remember thinking, $60.00; I am not going to buy any books. I can use this money for something better. Later I thought otherwise. Sandy was different. What would prompt a wealthy, white, suburban housewife and mother of four to impress herself upon me? I was curious to find out. Maybe there was something else to be gained in reading the listed books.

My purchase, reading and future discussions with Sandy over the content of the books were one of the wisest investments I have ever made. My follow up germinated our friendship and provided me with my first unadulterated look at white America up close and personal, guided by one of their own whose only desire was to remove the cloud shrouding my mind that I might be better informed.

In 1985 my father passed away. He was 57. In 1983 after he relocated to his home town I went to visit him because I had heard he was ill. My father was never a man of many words with me and very few words passed between us while I was there. We met in the parlor of his father's house. Upon his arrival we greeted one another and I asked how he was doing. He said that he was doing alright. He informed me he goes to see his doctor regularly, then he smiled. The rest of the time we sat in silence. Not once did he complain or make apologies for his life or circumstances. He took it in stride and made the best of it.

Very little was expected from me at the time of my father's passing. I wasn't consulted on anything. In my heart that seemed peculiar. My presence was noted and accepted and everything moved on. For me his passing was a heartfelt event. As I looked over him I couldn't help wondering who my father really was. The funeral itself was very nice. Many came amongst his family and friends to pay their last respects. I was pleased to hear during the eulogy that he had returned to the church before his passing. Though I believe my father was saddened over the course his life had taken, I can say he never presented his sadness to me. The quiet time we spent together in 1983 revealed the strength my father possessed in life in ways a mountain of words could never express.

In 1985 my grandfather, Shad was very ill. He was cared for at home by my aunt Eloise, my father's younger sister. Every morning she would tend to his every need from preparing his breakfast, to bathing and seeing to his over all hygiene. She would return periodically throughout the day to check on him and provide anything necessary. In the evening she would prepare his supper before preparing him for bed.

One day it was raining out and my grandfather got dressed grabbed a hoe and went out the back door of the house. I thought that odd. My aunt understanding my perplexed look smiled and encouraged him as he left. As I continued to watch from the back porch he began to whack at the weeds that had over grown in the no longer tended fields behind the house. After he tired he returned. My aunt assisted him as he undressed and fell into a comfortable sleep.

I was comforted over the fact that there was still enough love in my life that someone would give themselves to help another expecting nothing in return except gratitude. I was saddened that my generation seemed too preoccupied to provide that degree of compassion. I was glad my father during the last years of his life had a home he could return to.

The high ideals of HARK were a governing factor. Those ideals upheld and motivated the individual members of HARK. It was important that each member contribute to keep the community viable. Joseph Holland initiated his law practice and entered into real estate (R/E). James O'Neal created Legal Outreach, a not for profit organization established to address the barriers between the law and the urban youth. Leslie Walker went to work with the Harlem Urban Development Corporation Under the direction of Donald Cogsville. Dennis Henderson found a position in a downtown law office. I was invited by Joe to join him in real estate.

There are certain privileges you forfeit as a citizen once you are convicted of a felony. Many urban youth lose these privileges without ever realizing the opportunities lost because of criminal activity. Once lost some of these privileges are irretrievable, but remedies do exist to retrieve others.

Because of my criminal record I was ineligible to receive a sales person's license unless I was able to acquire a Certificate of Good Conduct issued by the Department of Parole. I never knew that policy existed. Research and the help of the members of HARK informed me of the threshold requirements. I had to be arrest free for 5 years. I had to maintain my own housing and I had to have good references.

Once acquired, the certificate clears your name and restores all lost privileges except work requiring the use of a gun and holding an elected public office. I met the bench mark, took the appropriate training, acquired my R/E sales person's license and went to work for African Caribbean and American Resources (ACAR) in Joe's law office.

Harlem's R/E boom was in its infancy. The speculators had come to town and were buying properties cheap to flip them for a quick profit. The change in the attitudes of the African American community coming out of the sixties with the riots and blackouts, the hike in the oil prices and increased cost in maintaining buildings, the drug scourge in Harlem and the flight of middle class Blacks had caused many landlords to abandon their properties. The City of New York had become the biggest landlord in town and was acquiring more properties through the In Rem process.

Slumlords were making headlines and the community politicos issued plans for the re-development of Harlem. Ed "Pork Chop" Davis wasn't buying any of it. Though in poor health, he mounted a response to bring current Harlem residents to the forefront of any plans developed. He saw the early stages of the re-development plan as a move by the powers that be with their back room deals to gentrify Harlem. He asserted that the current plans were an attempt to deny the current residents of the community an opportunity to benefit from the largest real estate deal in recent New York City history.

I thought I was faced with the opportunity of a lifetime. I thought R/E was a part of God's plan for my life. I had enough contacts in the community to gain an edge in the Harlem R/E market. All I had to do was seize the moment. It was not to happen. God had other plans.

HARK continued to grow and attract new members. It was during this period that I met Mimsie Robinson. When he first frequented HARK he was still a student of Brown University about to graduate. After graduation he joined

HARK and took up residence in our community quarters.

HARK was not comprised of a loose band of individuals going through life haphazardly. They were organized. They developed strategies to accomplish their goals. They researched and developed programmatic outreaches to provide information and service the needs of community residents. I found myself a committee member for many of the projects and assisted in their implementation as an ideologue and practitioner. I was provided an opportunity to perform with them and I took it. The bible studies continued on Thursdays where the truths of God were discussed and ideas were fostered. Street outreaches were planned and regularly scheduled. Food was prepared and made available for the hungry. Retreats were planned and strategies concretized.

In time Hark moved forward to implement a number of the envisioned projects. We fanned throughout the Harlem community. We formally introduced ourselves to various church pastors to gauge their interest in our ideas of ministry. It was a arduous and often disappointing task. Some were not interested. Some were interested, but lacked the resources and others just lacked faith.

In 1984 God opened a door in Bethel Gospel Assembly (BGA) under the pastorate of Reverend Ezra N. Williams. The church had recently purchased at auction an abandoned junior high school building from the city of New York. After 2 years of hard work, mostly using sweat equity and God's favor they opened the new facilities for worship. One of the members of Hark (Wayne) attended their services and informed us of this new church ministry. An exploratory team was sent out and returned with a good report. The pastor had expressed an interest in meeting with the members of Hark.

I was not present at the initial meetings, but they went very well. At later meetings, which I attended, I was floored by the openness and honesty revealed by the senior staff of the church. Pastor Ezra N. Williams, associate pastors Reverend Gordon Williams, Reverend Carlton T. Brown and the mission director Dr. Ruth Onukwe, attended the meetings on behalf of BGA. Here we all are in the back rooms of power discussing future possibilities. Usually in such settings there is a lot of allusion, sublime suggestion and posturing going on. None of this was evident amongst the BGA leadership. They all were straight forward and to the point.

The senior pastor made an offer after hearing our proposal for the implementation of a Christian counseling center operating within the context of the church setting. BGA under the guidance of the pastor would allocate space in the present facilities for the operation of the center. He would then introduce Hark to the congregation and raise the money for the renovation of the space to meet the specs and requirements necessary to operate the program effectively. After the completion of the renovations the church would supply the seed money to support the initial staffing of the center. In return Hark would have to provide the necessary staff and operate the counseling center. I had never in my entire life encountered such an open willingness on anyone's part before. God was truly moving.

I was impressed. If this was how the leadership in this church operated behind closed doors, what were they doing on Sundays? I ventured to see. In early 1985 I began attending Sunday services. At first I sat in the rear of the sanctuary. A good vantage point from which to see what was going on and if I picked up the wrong vibe I could ease out unnoticed. The services were well organized and the members devoted. The preaching was excellent. The messages from the pulpit were as if God was giving directives. I gradually moved from the rear to occupy a seat three rows from the front on the piano side. My bench buddy was mother Marguerite who has since gone on to be with the Lord.

I have always loved singing and that love was evident at Bethel during the worship services. The worship service began at 11:00 am and continued for one hour. Within that time the offering was collected. The worship prepared every heart to receive the spoken word presented by Rev. Ezra N. Williams. The greatest man I have yet met in Christ. His love for God and the people of God resonated through his delivery. I always felt, as did everyone else that God was speaking directly to me through his messages. I had found my church home.

Bethel made room for everyone. Its reason for being, missions. Its motto: Enter to learn and go forth to serve. Its method was love. Everyone was encouraged to get involved. Each member was responsible to God to perform a task for the up building of the Kingdom of God. There were no capital I's and no little u's. Each member could make an equal contribution and each one had an equal stake. I was able to commit myself fully to this cause.

While I was watching I was being watched. To become a member all potential candidates were required to attend the New Converts classes comprised of 8 lessons. It took approximately three months to complete the classes if you went consistently. It did not matter whether you were a new convert to the faith or not. The classes provided you with an opportunity to understand the theological foundations on which the church was standing. One informed member in agreement with your core beliefs is always better than having ten members without a clue.

In 1986 I became an official member of Bethel Gospel Assembly. In the mean time Rev. Williams followed through on all his promises. The doors of the Beth Hark Christian Counseling Center, Inc. opened its doors for the first time in April of 1985. As a member of HARK I was asked to sit on the board of directors. I knew it was the hand of God that had made all that I was experiencing possible. I looked back to see what He had done. God had encased me in Harlem's Ark of Freedom amongst the most reputable, socially speaking. These people were immediately given audience once they were introduced. I just tagged along for the ride. Their acceptance of me made me acceptable to others. HARK was my list of references. A bridge God established to allow me to cross and enter into mainstream Christianity. A body of believers I am still friends with until this day.

I was about to embark on another spiritual journey. At the completion of the New Converts classes I was baptized by water for the second time. My first baptism at the age of 9 didn't count because I didn't understand the faith. This time I was fully aware of what I was submitting to. Next I took the right hand of fellowship. After I joined the church I was asked by the Pastor to consider teaching the New Converts classes with Dr. Ruth on Thursday evenings. Me teach bible classes? It was one thing to host informal discussions; it was another thing altogether to stand in the position of the teacher. I decided to accept if I was allowed to take the classes again. The first time I took the classes as a student. This time I studied as a teacher in training.

At my trial instruction I was terrified. What if I didn't know the material? What if someone asked a question I did not have the answer to? What if someone disagreed with a position taken? What if? What if? What if? In faith I put my fears to the side and presented myself. God did the rest. I had a wonderful time before the class. The Spirit of the Lord moved. I evidenced the gift of teaching and had fun at the same time.

By June of 1987 things were going well all around. I was engaged in my life on all fronts. I managed three buildings and brokered a sale or purchase every once in a while. I had developed relationships with several speculators, property owners and R/E brokers in the community. I was shaking and making moves. I was on my way as far as R/E was concerned. Then the bottom fell out. A warrant dropped and I was arrested.

Officers from the warrant squad were staked out at my residence on 137th Street in HARK. Earlier in the day they had accosted Mimsie mistaking him for me. After proving his identity he was released. As I exited the building I saw the police eying me from their unmarked car. They pulled off and passed by me. My street instincts kicked in. As they passed I eyed them too, but I pretended I didn't see them. After they made their turn around the corner I knew I could double back to avoid them. I thought I had nothing to fear.

When the officers made their second pass they jumped out of their car, asked for my name, hand cuffed, searched me and carried me off to the 28<sup>th</sup> precinct. I didn't know what was going on. It was 1987. I had been crime free since March of 1981. What type of nonsense was this? Everything I had accomplished was at stake. If I wasn't available I feared all would be lost. All this effort couldn't amount to nothing. More immediate, Walter my youngest son was in daycare and I needed someone to pick him up and take care of him until I was released. In my frustration I angrily assaulted God in my heart. The last place I wanted to be was in jail. In my state of anger and helplessness God spoke. Walter, remember Joseph.

In all truth if you look to God He will give you a peace that surpasses all human understanding. Right there in the bullpens of the precinct I accepted my fate. I believed God just like in the biblical story of Joseph, God could allow me to be jailed unjustly. My being in jail didn't take anything away from the truths of God in the least. Was not God still God? And if it was His will for me to be in prison, had not I promised to serve Him? Couldn't God still get pleasure from my life if I remained faithful and obedient in jail? Acknowledging that my present circumstances were God ordained, I decided I would still serve Him, even from prison.

Rev. Gordon Williams arrived at the precinct within 2 hours to visit me before I was transported down town. I was moved that the church had shown a concern. No one in all my arrests had ever appeared at the precinct on my behalf before except my mother. I had flash backs of the bull pen experience. I asked Pastor Gordon to bring me a hero sandwich and some orange juice. He did. I had no desire to eat those sandwiches they used to serve or to go hungry. He inquired as to my circumstances. I told him everything I knew at the time. He prayed for my well being and protection and left.

Jail is a violent place. In the past I survived in part due to my own willingness to employ violence. This time the threat of violence as a shield of protection was not an option if I was going to remain faithful in my service to God. God demands humility and kindness as character traits, both are dangerous qualities to exhibit in the prison system. I was in no mood to be abused because I wanted to be a faithful Christian. This was something I would have to face very soon.

The bullpen experience was every bit as bad as I remembered it to be. The accommodations left much to be desired. The company, literally stinks, the atmosphere oppressive and the food not fit to eat. I think that is part of the plan. If you make the bullpen experience as horrific as possible it could discourage you from ever returning. After seeing the judge I was remanded to Riker's Island. It was just a matter of time before I would have to act.

After 2 days in the area where I was being housed my locker had been broken into several times during chow time. I was well aware of what was going on and I knew I couldn't allow this to continue. What could I do? I prayed and asked God for guidance. Taking notice of who was cliquing with whom, I decided to make a stand. I didn't know what God was going to do, but I knew what I had to do to put a stop to this.

I made it my business to stand at the end of the chow line as everyone was escorted out of the dormitory to the mess hall. I took a good look at the last few inmates who lagged behind. I moved to the front of the line as the correction officers escorted us. I finished eating quickly. I got at the front of the line on our return trip so I could be the first inmate to enter the dorm. My property, as I feared, was gone.

I had a good idea who did it and what crew he was running with. Now came the hardest part. Biding my time I cornered the suspected culprit. Looking him dead in the eye I informed him I knew it was him who stole my property. He looked back at me as intently and said, "You will have no more problems from me. You approached me like a man and will respect you as a man. I wasn't sure I could take him at his word and prepared myself for an assault.

Next I went over to the rest of the crew and addressed them all. I let them know I knew what they were up to and I wasn't going to tolerate them stealing from me. I told them that we were all in here together. I was not there to make a life for myself, but to do the best I could for myself to be released and to help others while I was there. If anybody had any issues with me come see me about them and we will take them from there. By the time I had finished speaking a crowd had gathered in the back of the dormitory. Everyone including myself expected trouble. No one said a word.

Later that evening another inmate had a concern about his case. He approached me about his problem. The solution was simple. I gave him my opinion and asked him if I could pray to God over his situation. He agreed. After praying one of the inmates from the thief's crew came over to me and apologized for the things they had taken and asked for my forgiveness, because he did not know that I was a man of God. Amazing, God had proven Himself again. The old adage of people taking kindness for weakness was destroyed.

My next hurdle was the case itself. I was prepared to remain in jail, but that wasn't my preference. I approached God about my concerns and He informed me to fight them all the way. I knew exactly what that meant and I knew exactly what to do. At my next court appearance I informed my attorney, Joseph Holland that I would be appearing before the grand jury on my behalf. I had never done that before. It was the wisdom of defense attorneys to dissuade defendants from appearing before the grand jury because the defendant's attorney is not allowed to represent you in the jury room. Nevertheless I heard what I heard from God.

At the appointed time I appeared before the grand jury. God was with me. I had that sense of peace and assurance I was becoming more familiar with from God. I knew everything was going to be all right. I returned to Rikers and continued serving God. A couple of weeks later my name was broadcast over the prison loud speaker, Walter Wilson, on the bail. I wasn't sure if I had heard correctly. I knew I didn't have enough money to make bail, but they did call my name. I went to inquire at the front booth to be sure. Yep, they called me out for bail. As I was being processed I learned I hadn't made bail after all. I was being released by the grand jury, no true bill. I was in awe of God. I never knew God was so real.

God had gotten my full attention. It was time for me to change the course of my life again. After my release I submitted an application to Baruch College. I shifted my focus from a business in R/E to full time ministry. I tossed my concerns over my age and being in college with people 10 or more years younger than myself. Again my fears were irrational. I flourished. I graduated in 1990 with honors. My mother was thrilled.

While in college I gave my full attention to Bethel. I stopped attending the community meetings and dealing with most secular matters. I remained on the board of Beth Hark and Legal Out Reach with James O'Neal and Bethsheba Cooper. I moved out of the HARK residence. I took up residence once again with my mother with no qualms whatsoever.

My mother and I learned to enjoy each others company and conversation. She told me about her childhood and moving to Savannah GA from Camilla; how she felt about her being born out of wedlock. She told me about getting to know my paternal grandfather and why she married my father. My mother and I never talked much together before this time. To me she was the determined silent type. Silent as she was, she was reflective.

My mother had a difficult time growing up. In her time being born out of wedlock made you a social outcast and openly referred to as a bastard. My mom hated that word. As a child she was a hard worker and pretty tough. If you were in her age range you got the opportunity to call her that name once. After that freebie she would see to it that you wouldn't have the nerve to do it again.

When my mother moved to Savannah she met my father and his family. My mother used to help my paternal grandfather, Shad, harvest his crops. He and his family lived at 3908 3$^{rd}$ Street in a house he built with his own hands. She told me he was very nice. He used to always give her some extra collard greens. She liked my father because he was funny and kind. She told me how she had to fend for herself when she was a pre and early teen. There were plenty of older lecherous men about trying to take advantage of her. She was adept at spotting and avoiding them.

My favorite story was how she and my father planned their escape from Georgia. My mother was the more adventurous one. She told me that my father and she agreed that he would leave to go to New York first. He was to find a job, a place for them to stay and then send for her. When she arrived they would get married and start their family. She wanted a large family. It was her intent to have 12 children, but she settled for six. Anyway my father left as planned without anyone knowing where he was going except for her. He soon sent for her and the rest is history. She was only 18 years old.

My paternal aunts and uncles are Dennis, Leroy, Marion, Randolph, Eloise and Rose. My maternal aunts and uncles are Leola, Hazel, Claretha, Genovia, Kelly and Willie. From their issue I have a host of 1st cousins living throughout the United States.

My mother was somewhat saddened by life. She didn't complain about it, but things didn't turn out as well for her as she had hoped. She received too many hurts and not enough help from those she relied upon. My mother wanted to complete her high school education. She told me of the time she insisted on going to school when she was eleven years old. At the time she had only completed the third grade before moving to Savannah because she always had to help her mother out around the house and go out to work because she was the oldest.

In Savannah when she did return to school she was so embarrassed because all the other kids her age had more schooling than she had. When she was asked what grade she was up to, she told them the sixth grade. She told me she worked so hard to catch up, which she did. She received excellent grades by the end of the school season. She wanted to continue school at the time, but had to leave again to help provide for her family. What a time of healing and restoration. What a time of getting to know my mother. What a time of help I provided for her. What a time of loving the Lord.

In 1988 I was appointed director of Beth Hark Christian Counseling Center replacing Mary Ann Royal the first director. I had entered full time ministry. In 1990 I was ordained under the United Pentecostal Council of the Assemblies of

God (U.P.C.A.G.). In that same year I graduated with honors from Baruch College. Each semester I received a scholarship after making the honor roll.

God had proven Himself to be in the life changing business. Just a few years earlier I was a career criminal. I lived my life on the borders of society. I had no desire to know, much less serve God. But God rescued me from my ignorance. The journey was not easy. Neither was the journey over. I would not wish what I had to go through on anyone. But if that is what God had required for me, it was in my best interest to go through it all for the life I had and for my life to come.

The final major area that I was impressed to deal within my life was parenting. I needed to develop individual, personal relationships with all my children. Since the time I came to know God personally I made a concerted effort to be involved in their lives. All three of my children presented a unique set of issues I needed to confront. The primary issues revolved around my absence during their formative years. Secondly each of my children had a different mother that I was not involved with, neither was I going to be involved with any of them again.

I truly believe there is a natural desire in all children to want to be loved and cared for by their natural parents if possible. I know it was true in my own case. Not having that love or knowing it can breed emotional distress and erect a wall bricked with a lack of trust as a barrier between you and your deserving child.

At first Walter III my youngest was the easiest of the three to connect with. He was born in 1980. I was involved in his life from the beginning. Believing I had a handle on him I reached out to my oldest, Tesha. I started to make my presence felt with her after I returned from prison in 1977. I would see her and talk to her and give her a few dollars from time to time. After my conversion I better grasped the depth of my obligation to her as her father.

Tesha was raised by her maternal grandmother after the death of her mother in 1975. I was incarcerated at the time. Ms. Margorie Mance, Stephanie's mother raised Tesha as her own daughter and loved her unconditionally. That love afforded my daughter a degree of stability, which is evident to this day, but growing up in the projects presented their own challenges.

Tesha is what I called a tough cookie. She was ready to fight at the drop of a hat. Yet I saw she possessed a lot of fear and insecurity and still needed support and encouragement. Together with her younger sister Lacresia (Cree) my concerns only multiplied. Prayer was my constant companion and patience my guide. I did all I knew to reach her. She was cautious and wary. I persisted in my pursuit and display of my love and concern.

It took a long time for the wall between us to come completely down and permit me to establish myself in her life as a man she could trust and respect as her father. My pursuit of my daughter went cross-country as she grew older. At 18 she married a wonderful man from South Carolina, Marcus McMinn and moved away. He was in the military. Every place of residence my daughter relocated to because of her husband's military service I made it my business to visit her. We maintained our long distance relationship. It was a joy to see my daughter come to maturity. It was a greater joy to see her grow as a wife and parent. She has given birth to three wonderful children (Marquise, Markell and Tiara). As a mother she has protected them from the disappointments she suffered in her early childhood.

The last major barrier between my daughter and I was demolished one winter while she was living in Fort Stewart, GA. She had said something over the phone that upset me. She had gone too far. In my mind that was enough. I informed her I was on my way and we would have it out when I got there. In a dispute I prefer a face to face confrontation. My daughter is out spoken, so I prepared for the worst. That very day I jumped into my car and drove straight to Georgia.

When I arrived at Tesha's house my youngest sister, Felecia was there. She drove in from Atlanta to meet me when I arrived. I was caught unawares. My daughter was all smiles and hugs. My true education on women was about to begin. I was blind to the female point of view. Where was the anger? Where was the venom? I am in tune with the masculine perspective of things, but women leave me wondering. I wasn't sure what to expect next. After a few more smiles and pleasantries our three way discussion began.

They double teamed me and I told them so. They assured me that was not happening. I did not know how to process that information. It looked like double-teaming. It sounded like double-teaming. It felt like double-teaming. But they said it was not double-teaming.

At that point as a man you call them a bunch of lying heifers or worse, curse them out and walk away, but something else was going on. I knew I had to try to grasp where they were coming from. I knew they were trying to tell me something because of their love and concern for me, but I wasn't getting it. They employed too many words. That was information overload. They were trying to appeal to my heart and head at the same time. This was not the first time these two put me through something like this. The last time I wrote my experience with them off as female mumbo jumbo. This time would not be like before. This time things would be different. I couldn't dismiss them. I strained to understand what they had to say.

They schooled me on women. They talked about intonations and other subtleties women employ. They talked about things I needed to be on the lookout for from other women, as well as themselves. They told me about things that their own husbands are not aware of. It was almost like learning to speak another language. Slowly I began to grasp their point of view. My daughter and sister were speaking out of their pain and experiences. I was a man. They wanted me to hear them and respect them for what they had to say and for who they were. I was supposed to be on their side to protect them when I could. It was made clear to me on that day that no matter how old my daughter was, she was always going to be my daughter. She wanted and appreciated me in her life and nothing I did was supposed to interfere with that. If it did I was supposed to see and address it head on.

I got it. I had the wrong idea. I was wrong on two levels. 1) I believed after your children reach adulthood they were on their own. True, but not really. After they reach adulthood only my responsibility to provide for them changes, everything else remains the same. 2) As a father I was supposed to keep my relationship with my children as a priority in my life. Anything new that developed in my life had to be measured against the impact it would have on my children first. Yea, I was grown and the father, but I wasn't free to do anything I wanted. My ignorance of this feminine perspective of life had brought about a lot of emotional distress in my sister's and daughter's lives and therefore my own.

My second child, Lamar brought the greatest pain to my heart. Lamar was raised by my sister Betty as her own from birth. Every advantage available was afforded him wrapped around her love. My son like all my children was exceptionally bright and very talented. As I was getting more involved in his life tragedy struck on December 8, 1991. That Sunday Lamar was shot and killed by an acquaintance at the tender age of 17. The aftermath of that day still reverberates to this day.

At the time of the incident I felt abandoned by God. Here I was in church all day about God's business, mind you. All the while my son was out in the streets being murdered. Where was God? I had no sense or inclination that my child was in trouble. Why didn't God let me know?

Later that evening my family finally was able to reach me at the church. I received a message to call my sister Betty. When I called I spoke to my sister's husband, Ernest. We call him Butch. He informed me that Lamar had been shot. After the initial shock I asked him how Lamar was doing. Butch said," He is not."

My sister Betty was the hardest hit by this tragedy. A mother's pain at the loss of her child is hard for me to gauge. I took a back seat at the time of her grief and prayed to God to comfort her. In time I received some comfort from God on the matter because I had spent quality time with my son during the last years of his life. It also came home that long life is not guaranteed and tragedy befalls us all.

Eventually problems erupted between Walter's mother and me. I felt he was being used as a pawn between us. Allegations of abuse and parental neglect began to fly in every direction. The Bureau of Child Welfare (BCW) got involved and things worsened. My son was caught in the middle forced into court and bounced from pillar to post in foster care. I was arrested for being a negligent parent. All the while my son was left parentless because he couldn't return to his mother's either.

I was indignant. I was being accused of being a neglectful father. That was ridiculous. My court appointed attorney advised me to accept a plea to a lesser charge. I refused. I insisted on going to trial. I wanted my name to be cleared. The case lingered for months. Each court date was consistently postponed for one reason or another by the prosecution. It became very frustrating.

Eventually all the charges were dropped and the arrest was expunged from my record. My son returned to my care. It was obvious the damage had been done. The trauma my son suffered through that experience would take years to overturn. Whether God performed a miracle or allowed the natural processes to take their course, I was going to be there for and with him as his father.

I learned and changed a lot during this period of my life walking with God. I had matured spiritually. With each crisis, set back and experience I grew in my understanding of God. My mother moved out of the Saint Nick and into a co-op in the Bronx. I remained in the 240 apartment. My son and I had our own apartment. Things were looking up. In November of 1991 my wife, Diane returned. We renewed our relationship and prepared to face life's challenges together.

The power of a man in parenting is grossly understated in today's world. Over a ten-year period I have had the privilege to see and experience the difference a man makes as a father in the lives of his children. I know the quality of the lives of all my children improved because I made myself accessible to them. The quality of the life for my grandchildren is better because of the influence I had in my children's lives. It feels good knowing I contributed to their improved well being.

The power of a man is also apparent amidst women. Women have an innate need to believe in men. If a woman can find a man she can believe in she would sacrifice who she is for him. If disappointed that need generally degenerates. It is then expressed at its best between tolerance and apathy. At its worst her need falls between bitter disappointment and distain. I learned this from the women in my life.

My exposure to other women brought this eye opener. Seeing what men and women go through in their relationships with one another. The bitterness expressed, hearing a woman's dissatisfaction with the man in her life. The failure of so many marriages and the break up of so many homes give evidence that something is seriously wrong. The hurt I experienced in women I related to, that was already evident in them long before I was an issue in their lives. The many conversations I have had with women as they tried to explain to me what was missing in their lives. My sisters testify to this. The evidence is everywhere.

My mother was deeply wounded by my father's inability to deliver on his promises to her as a wife and mother. It had a profound effect on her. At the time I was too young to fully appreciate the happenings, but after I grew older and especially after I returned to live with my mother in 1988 it was made quite clear in no uncertain terms.

My mother was no slouch. She was quite capable of taking care of herself. But when I proved myself responsible, she had no hesitation in relinquishing much she could do herself into my hands. I could sense the comfort she received knowing her son was taking care of things for her in her willingness to share with me what she was thinking of doing.

My daughter and youngest sister I would have to say were the most influential in coming to some measure of my understanding women. They violently fought for my concern and attention. They went to great lengths to force me to reconsider the ignorance of my ways. They were so happy as I slowly began to comprehend what they were talking about. There efforts were catalytic. Their time and attention sparked my desire to look at and pull together the pieces of my heart and mind to create a coherent outlook. I began to open up and allow women into spaces of my life I began to realize were present and accessible. It tickles me today as I look back at how one sided I was in my ignorance. No wonder I had so many problems with women.

I loved my wife Diane. Yet when she asked me to leave I had to get over her. I left her to her own devices and moved on. I wasn't in her face. I didn't try to woo her back. I came to accept everyone could not see me and my life the way I saw it. James O'Neal opened my eyes to that truth in 1984. If Diane couldn't see it I should not alter my course. Maybe she would see it in time. I just went about improving my character and quality of my life. She came back. Whatever happened to me as a man was enough to draw her back. She was all smiles and all was forgiven.

In today's world not enough men rise to the level they must entertain for a woman to command her belief in him. I received no positive instruction or direction in the matter whatsoever. I, like so many men, was too bogged down in my own selfishness to comprehend a woman's need. I tended to make light of women in my day-to-day intercommunications, but the gender bond will not be denied.

My resolve not to take advantage of a woman that expressed an interest in me became a plus. That and my being honest enough with them and me improved their trust and respect for me immeasurably. As I improved in character and nature so did my attractiveness to women. Finding a woman was no longer my problem; respecting them and learning how to keep my own impulses at bay became the issue.

There is something deep and real within human relationships and family bonds. This reality can either be of benefit to those connected or harmful. Too often in the past human interactions were harmful because of what I as an adult failed to do or take responsibility for. I was given a second chance. I took advantage of that chance and the lives of the people I am most accountable to and responsible for have been immeasurably improved.

A man with a pure heart and a desire to love commands a lot of power over the lives of other people. God released that power into my hands and taught me responsibility.

I promised God I would serve Him for 13 years as I had the devil. In return if God could do me better than the devil in that amount of time I would serve Him the rest of my life. God beat the devil in 7.

Harlem's Ark of Freedom

254

Top- Legal Outreach, James O'neil, Bethsheba     Cooper, Dennis Henderson
      Bottom- Sandy Van Dyk with sons     and a friend

The People of the State of New York

To All to Whom These Presents Shall Come:

Greeting:

Whereas    Walter Wilson             was convicted in the courts indicated below of the of the following offenses for which he received the sentence set forth:

| OFFENSE | COURT OF CONVICTION | DATE OF SENTENCE | SENTENCE |
|---|---|---|---|
| Criminal Possession Stolen Property, 3rd | New York Criminal Court | 2/18/70 | 6 months |
| Criminal Mischief, 3rd | New York Criminal Court | 2/18/70 | 6 months |
| Possession Dangerous Weapon | New York Criminal Court | 11/6/70 | 6 months |
| Att. Petit Larceny | New York Criminal Court | 8/25/71 | 6 months |
| Robbery, 2nd | New York Supreme Court | 2/18/76 | XXX/4-0-0 |
| Criminal Possession of a Controlled Substance, 5th | New York Supreme Court | 5/4/76 | 2-0-0/4-0-0 |
| Criminal Possession of a Controlled Substance, 7th | New York Criminal Court | 4/9/75 | Time Served |
| Possession of a Hypodermic Instrument | New York Criminal Court | 12/15/73 | Time Served |

Whereas, in accordance with the provisions of law, the Board of Parole has verified that the person aforesaide has maintained a record of good conduct since December 15, 1979    and is a fit person to receive this grant;

Therefore, Know Ye That we have granted unto    Walter Wilson this Certificate of Good Conduct for the following purpose: to    remove all legal bars and disabilities to employment, license and privilege except those imposed by Sections 265.01(4) and 400.00 of the Penal Law and except the right to hold Public Office.

[X] This certificate shall be considered permanent.

[ ] This certificate shall be considered temporary until _____. After this date, unless revoked earlier by the parole board, this certificate shall be considered permanent. A person who knowingly uses or attempts to use a revoked certificate in order to obtain or exercise any right or privilege that he would not be entitled to obtain or to excercise without valid certificate shall be guilty of a misdemeanor.

| Signature of issuing official(s) | Print or type name(s) | Title(s) |
|---|---|---|
| *[signature]* | Ronald A. Hotaling | Executive Secretary Board of Parole |
| NYSIO No. 3044147 J | Issue Date January 23, 1986 | Revision Date |

Complete the following for DCJS, only if fingerprints are not obtainable

Certificate of good conduct; removes legal bars to      employment

256

Continuing Education
SCHOOL OF GENERAL STUDIES
OFFICE OF THE DEAN

(212) 690-6611

July 22, 1985

Dear Student:

Re.  Real Estate Salesperson License Course.

Congratulations on your successful completion of the Real Estate Salesperson License
course and the passing of your final examination.

Enclosed you will find two certificates.  The Certification of Satisfactory Completion must be mailed by you directly to the Department of State. Students who
presently possess a provisional license need only send that certificate and a cover
letter to the address indicated.  Students seeking to be newly licensed should obtain an application form from the local office of the Department of State (located
at 270 Broadway in New York City; telephone 212/587-5687),then mail the form, plus
the appropriate fee, along with the certificate to the Albany address. Please note
the following: (1) the application form must be signed by a sponsoring broker;
(2) the original certificate must be sent to Albany; copies are not acceptable;(3)
you will be informed by the Department of State that you are required to pass a
test at one of their offices before your license is finally approved.  To the best
of our knowledge this information is accurate.

Best wishes in your career.

Sincerely

*Larry J. Barr*

Larry J. Barr
Real Estate Program Coordinator

Real Estate Salesperson license letter of            completion

# The City College of New York
## School of General Studies
### Division of Continuing Education

# This Certificate Is Awarded
to

Walter Wilson

### For Completion of

Real Estate Salesperson

on this ___10th___ day of ___July___ 19_85_.

_Norman P. Shapiro_
**Director, Division of Continuing Education**

_Reuben S. Schofield_
**Course Instructor**

Certificate of completion- Real Estate Sales

Process Server's license

Lamar before he passed away with Earnest 'Butch'
Dickerson, my sister Betty's husband

Top- Tesha , all grown up with husband Marcus        and children
Middle- College graduation
Bottom- Marcus and Tesha, happily married

261

Top- my grandmother, Weldon Cunningham

Bottom- grandmother, my mother and her       sisters, and my sister Rebecca

Out with my brothers, Sammy's on City     Island

My mother and her Spicer siblings, Ulysses and          Mamie

# Chapter Seven

Who knew life could be so fulfilling? What was wrong with me? I couldn't believe I wouldn't believe in God sooner. The life I had acquired through Christ was good. It was unbelievable. I did not have all I wanted, but everything I did have, I found pleasure and satisfaction with. It wasn't a quest for material gain, but a desire to be pleasing to God and attain peace in and around me. It was a quest for righteousness.

Who knew God was ever present and real. I had changed because of God. I had overcome my fears in life by His power. If God is real and the power of God is real as the Bible says, why is there not more evidence of His reality amongst the people? Why weren't we evidencing the promises of God? The power of God can not be denied. When God is present His power is present.

I recall a day in the summer of 1978. On this beautiful day five drug dealers happened to meet on the corner of 134th Street and 7th Ave. by chance. We all had recently purchased new cars. I was present along with my brother, L.A., Martini and the Indian. As we pulled up and exited our vehicles every eye on the avenue turned their attention to us. We weren't paying any attention to them, but I noticed the admiration and respect we commanded in our show of prosperity. If we as men of crime could elicit such a response, how much more would God elicit for Himself through us that believe, than men who believed in selling dope?

Entering Bethel was like entering another world. It was a self-contained, self maintained and self sustained institution. Within the United Pentecostal Council of the Assemblies of God (UPCAG) Bethel had become a dominant influence under the pastorate of Reverend Ezra N. Williams. The UPCAG like Bethel was founded out of rejection. In 1906 the Pentecostal movement was initiated under the leadership of Rev. William Seymour on Azusa Street in California. His efforts immediately launched a new movement. Two new denominations emerged, the Church of God in Christ and the Assemblies of God after a few years. A coalition of newly found fellowships under the Pentecostal movement petitioned the Assemblies of God to join and was denied. It was suspected their denied membership was due to race. This rejection persuaded them to form their own denominational church fellowship. Bethel Gospel Assembly was one of those churches.

The birth of Bethel followed a similar experience. Two women of color from Harlem visited a church in midtown Manhattan. Both women accepted Christ during a service, but were not allowed to join the fellowship. A woman by the name of Lillian Kraeger who was White and a member of the Midtown Manhattan fellowship learned of the plight of these two women and offered to disciple them in Harlem if they would invite their friends to the meetings she would host in their homes. Out of these gatherings Bethel Gospel Assembly was founded around 1916. The fellowship grew and functioned without a pastor for several years. The first pastor of the Church was Rev. Barsey. He served as Pastor for 40 years. Rev. Williams assumed the pastorate in 1966.

The influence of Bethel was far reaching – touching the Caribbean, Central America, Canada, Africa, India and China. Its greatest influence was spread and felt in Harlem and around the City of New York. Pastor Williams was serving in the office of a bishop when I became a member in 1986, that same year Reverend Ezra N. Williams was officially ordained a bishop within the UPCAG.

The heart of Bethel exuded through Bishop Ezra N. Williams. He made everyone seem important.

All his efforts and energies were directed towards pleasing God in advancement of the Kingdom. Both his eyes and mind were sharp. He was always on the lookout and sensitive to the called and willing to serve. The spirit he carried and the integrity that accompanied it was exhibited amongst his church leadership. His leaders were extensions of his service and like him they were on the lookout. They got to observe and know everyone who frequented the fellowship. Under their direction the church was embraced within a blanket of love and concern.

BGA was growing because it was serious about taking care of God's business. Rev. Carlton Brown presided over the youth ministries. Rev. Gordon Williams provided leadership over church worship. Rev. Dr. Lillian Chapell provided leadership over Christian education and Dr. Ruth Onukwe presided over the missions department, the purpose of the church. It was within this envelope I was able to find my ministerial 'niche'.

The historical core for membership was of Caribbean descent. Many of its current members were direct descendants of the founding members of Bethel. Several others were recruits of the initial crusades to Aruba that were sponsored by Pastor Williams and the numerous street

crusades that followed. There were the
Boatswains, the Juliens, the Cudjoes, the
Williams, the Patricks, the Phipps, Kenneth
Williams, Mae and Conrad Grant, Dudley
Stewart and his family, Roy Boston and his
family, the Burrells, Michael Desmond
Hickinson, Sister Ruth Harper, Wesley Streeter,
Alvin Forde, Henrietta Clark, Beverly, Valerie
and Mother Washington, Mother Hunt, Mother
Dean, Judith Pemberton, Victor Letren, Sister
Beth Greenaway, and Sister Stephanie Kirnon.
These are just a few of the devoted and faithful of
the rank and file membership of Bethel Gospel
Assembly. Each member had their own
personality and brought their unique gifts and
talents to give Bethel its distinction.

Within the church I learned about revivals,
awakenings and denominationalism. I could see
the imprint of their posterity operating in society
at large. I began to understand that the world we
live in has been influenced by the Church for the
good, more than we care to acknowledge.

I have always had dreams. In the past,
immediacy and the practicalities of life got in the
way of my dreams and suppressed them. My
dreams revolve around a strong sense of justice.
Whether my sense of justice is innate or grafted

269

in I don't know. What I do know is this, my sense of justice is rarely observed operating within life.

My early socialization, home, school, church and early  TV tended to reinforce my sense, if not nurture my sense of justice. Reality on the other hand flat out denied it especially amongst Blacks and other minorities in America.

The civil rights era resonated with my young soul. It appeared as an effort to right the blatant injustices of White America against African Americans. We as a nation were given an opportunity to approach social righteousness and failed. As suddenly as the era presented itself it faded away. A few assassinations and the movement lost its way. The hard earned rights achieved were hijacked by other groups to advance their own causes.

advance their own causes.

I wondered what had happened. Why didn't those who followed pick up the cause and lead us the rest of the way?  Some saw progress and so did I. Others were disappointed and so was I. Life is funny that way. With all that was gained and all that was lost justice is still denied.

God has raised me above my own need to act against alleged injustices. Before I knew Christ a

lot of who I had become was derived from my
belief that life was unfair. My faith allowed me to
realize that God is just. In spite of all I see or
don't see God is the righteous judge. Everyone
will be judged on every word that has proceeded
out of their mouths. There is nothing hidden that
will not be brought to light. With that burden
lifted I was free to look after my own deficiencies.
Having addressed my own shortcomings with
the help of God I began to hope and dream again.
I also realized that one's quest to end
shortcomings is a never ending struggle. Close
one eye and they threaten to return with a
vengeance.

Bethel afforded an environment where my
dreams and hopes were nurtured and allowed to
grow. I, along with my dreams and hopes, grew
mentally and spiritually. It was not long before I
was evidencing realized hopes with the
encouragement of BGA.

In 1988 I was given the directorship of Beth Hark
Christian Counseling Center (BHCCC). I had no
formal administrative training and it was my
first ministerial job, or any other job for that
matter, that operated on a 9 to 5 basis since the
summer of 1984. God proved His presence in my

life again as I took the helm of the counseling center.

The first day I took control I reviewed all the administrative materials to get a feel for how the center flowed administratively. I needed to understand what things needed to be done and when they needed to be done. I thought that it would take a week or two before I had a command of the office allowing me the room I needed to grasp the counseling aspects of the center.

On my second day circumstances demanded that I begin counseling. Again the presence of the Lord was with me. As it turned out I found that I was both a gifted administrator and counselor. I was given a new understanding. My years on the street were not entirely wasted or in vain. My selling drugs had honed my administrative and people skills. Working with the community organizations and HARK fine tuned those skills and assisted in developing my character. All that remained was a Godly setting to express these gifts and qualities in. If I could embody all of that into love perhaps I would leave a godly impression on someone's life.

Over my years in Christ I had to come to grips with the error of my ways. I learned where I went wrong. I learned why I went wrong. I watched the hand of God work within me to bring me to a place of victory over my shortcomings which were many. My misunderstandings of life led me to make wrong choices.

All life's difficulties are derived from sin. Every problem that anyone has is a result of some misunderstanding they have with godliness. Having a working knowledge of the word of God, and with the help of the Spirit of God, my deliverance experience provided a template of wisdom to guide others towards a path of righteousness.

My gifts made room for me. As director of Beth Hark CCC I was presented with the privilege and honor to occupy the pulpit. BGA scheduled an anniversary service for BHCCC. I was asked to prepare a message for the morning service and an anniversary program for the afternoon service. No one else approached me after I was given the assignment with any other instructions. I was allowed to present whatever was placed upon my heart. In truth I wasn't clear on what was in my heart or how it would come across.

The day arrived. I stood before a thousand people and by the grace of God I preached. I found out that day I was a gifted preacher. I had value. I was a little unorthodox and a little non-traditional, but gifted and anointed none the less. My public apprehensions began to dissolve.

Why did I consider myself to be unorthodox and nontraditional? Right is right and wrong is wrong. Before Christ I had thoughts, feelings, attitudes and behaviors that the Word of God challenged as I read. For me to obtain the promises of goodness God expresses in the Bible those thoughts, feelings, attitudes and behaviors had to be faced, overcome and replaced. I struggled for years to bring about the changed person God says He requires me to be in righteousness.

There were no two ways about it. Believe me I tried to find other ways to satisfy God, but I found none. If I wanted what God was offering in my life I had to reject the things that were in my life, that God rejected. The things being rejected refused to leave without a fight. I had to pay a price. My thoughts, feelings, attitudes and behaviors did not dissipate over night. I had to make a serious and determined effort. Once they were dismissed new possibilities were introduced to me that made available the offerings of God. I couldn't argue with it, debate it, dispute it or

disagree with it. It is what it is. I preached it like
I saw it. That's all I know.

I thank God for the leadership of BGA. They were
sensitive enough to the Spirit of God to recognize
a work God was performing in me that I was not
aware of at the time. The Bishop said of me at
one time, "You never know the flavor of the tea in
a bag until you place it in hot water. God has
placed Brother Walter in some hot water; the
aroma and flavor of God in Brother Walter smells
and tastes good." I broke down in tears. Someone
had shown appreciation for me for who I was and
not for what they could get.

In 1992 my mother-in-law, Wilma Thomas
passed away. Wilma was full of life and enjoyed
every day of it. She had a warm heart and
thrived in the company of other people. Wilma's
passing introduced a new level of consideration
afforded to me. I was asked by my wife to
oversee the arrangements for her mother's
funeral. Everyone else concerned was in
agreement. Mrs. Thomas' home going took place
at Bethel and I presided. It was a new
experience. I had to take responsibility for a
person who I only knew as an adult all of my life.
As the proceedings took place, everyone was
looking to me to provide what was appropriate

and to comfort those saddened. I placed my confidence in God to meet their every need. After the service was completed I passed into a new level of respect in the eyes of people I had known for most of my life.

These fresh experiences in ministry were just the beginning. God continued to develop my character. BHCCC grew under my leadership. BGA continually increased its contributions to the center and its staffing to meet the needs of the community we served. The reputation of the church grew and spread within the city.

I worked closely with Sister Judith Pemberton in the operation of the center. Sister Judy is fully devoted to her call and service to God. In her devotion she carries with her some rough edges that are freely expressed through her wit and vim. You can find her everyday completely immersed in the house of God serving in the Center, the kitchen or the sanctuary during the noon day prayer services. She has mounted after hour prayer ministries and a ministry of helps in the community. On Saturdays she is present as a staunch supporter of the church's street out reach ministry.

Judy is the type of member needed to support the vision of a church. She is also the type of

Christian needing a buffer from time to time.
Upon meeting her I noted if I could get along
with her I would be able to get along with anyone
in the church.

Tsa Ali-Peralte is another member of the staff of
Beth Hark. She is a fire and brimstone believer.
Her commitment to evangelism is
unquestionable. Her desire is to complete the
work God started in her through Master
Builders, a ministry designed to take the values
of the Christian faith into the public school
system.

Rev. Alberto Davila rounded out the counseling
staff. He is a gentle soul until riled. God has
humbled him and given him a spirit of patience.
Rev. Alberto has a tremendous testimony. Along
with his ministry to his family and Beth Hark he
is developing the Spanish speaking fellowship of
Bethel. Danette Codjoe was later added as my
administrative assistant. They, with the other
administrative staff and volunteers, fulfill the
duties of God to those in need through Beth Hark
Christian Counseling Center.

I continued to teach New Converts class. In time
I became very comfortable as a teacher and adept
at managing the  classroom. The Spirit of God
never failed to equip me to handle all matters

whether from a difference of opinion to fielding questions unrelated to the subject matter of the night. I came to look forward to my time in the classroom imparting knowledge to the newly saved and the hungry in Christ.

In 1991 Bethel inaugurated Discipleship a men's residential facility on the lower level of the church. The ministry was run by Rev. Leander Harris and his wife Yolanda. I was involved from the beginning in the operation of this ministry. Rev. Lee proved to be proficient in commanding respect and allegiance from the men who were seeking assistance within the ministry. It was a joy to see my church open its doors and provide a safe haven for men who had lost their way.

Beth Hark and Discipleship labored together as sister ministries. The counseling center provided personal guidance and direction; the church provided a worship experience in the midst of a fellowship; B.G.A. provided the financial support necessary to sustain 15 men in recovery and Rev. Lee secured everything else. It was a model that has preserved the lives and nurtured the souls of innumerable men.

In 1991 I was appointed president of Men in Ministry, the men's prayer group within Bethel. I came to realize I truly have a heart for men. It is my belief that Black men in particular are not provided with the social and cultural instruction and support necessary for them to assume their natural responsibilities. I know I didn't receive that instruction. I know I was deprived and I believe I know and understand why it was done.

I was socially nurtured under the same instruction of the average African American male. I am understood by Black males and I understand other Black males. I understand the house Negro and the field Negro. I understand the successful Negro and the ne're-do-well Negro. I understand the failed Negro. I have been most of them at one point or another in my life. I wasn't fulfilled as any of them.

Like me they need to be weaned off the illusion of what has been sown into our spirits by the world. I dreamed with the help of God that we would be supplied with the  wherewithal to realize who we are and what we need to do in Christ to bring about greater improvement amongst ourselves. The corrupt influences consuming the Black male are at the center of many of our problems. Search the hearts and faces of women and children and you will see the suffering and pain etched upon them due to male neglect. This is a stronghold of the devil.

That is a spiritual truth. If you want to improve something you must come to understand what is wrong with it. Analyzing the problem provides leads necessary to make alterations. Life is about God's love displayed through kindness, respect and consideration for humanity and the planet we live on. Self victimization, social exploitation and spiritual dehumanization are super-imposed on the back of humanity, especially the African American male. Our enslavement is due to ignorance. Love is the only property available to us to turn its tide. I applied it to the men.

Humanity comes first because we directly impact ourselves and those around us. We also have an impact on the physical world both naturally and spiritually. Every problem we face is because of who and what we are or are not. If we are not willing to first address ourselves and the error within ourselves then nothing will ever change for the better. I have heard that the definition of insanity is doing the same thing the same way over and over again and expecting a different result.

Early in life I made some decisions. I regarded them as good decisions because of the immediate gratification I received. Nothing at the time convinced me otherwise. It turned out that they were not good decisions. The future consequences brought depravity into the lives of everyone associated with me including family, friends and community. Believing I was right did not make me right. As a man God showed me my wrongs. Those wrongs were addressed and I am a better person for it. The lives of everyone around me are improved because of the change for the better that has occurred in me. If it worked for me it can work for others in the same fashion.

An empowered Black man is a scary thought for everyone. The fear of an empowered Black man has the potential to upset the status quo. What Black Man hasn't gotten on an elevator and felt a woman cringe, or found it difficult to catch a cab on a busy street, or maybe felt eyes on you as you were shopping at a department store. God is not a discerner of persons neither has He given us a spirit of fear. An empowered Black man in truth is no threat to anyone who is just. On the contrary an empowered Black man is the answer to many of the social problems facing our world today.

My leadership over the men's fellowship of Bethel was the door God opened before me to observe and understand ministry on a city wide and national level. Harlem was the preeminent Black community in America located in the preeminent city in America, New York. Whether real or imagined many eyes look to N.Y.C. to gauge the national pulse and to gain influence in international arenas or to just increase their fame and fortune.

In the early 90's a new move had taken root in Christian America. It was the Christian men's movement. The recognized father of the movement was Dr. Edwin Louis Cole the founder of the Christian Men's Network. For decades Dr. Cole had seeded the soil for men in Christianity both nationally and internationally. From his seedlings erupted Promise Keepers. This Ministry was taking America by storm. Under the direction of Andy Puleo, the regional director of The Navigators, an effort was launched to bring Promise Keepers into the New York area.

In '94 or '95 the Bishop received an invitation to attend a meeting for pastors and other church leaders to take place in a Harlem restaurant. The meeting was being hosted by Promise Keepers. As president of the men's fellowship my pastor asked me to attend. At the time I had not heard of them. Copelands (a popular Harlem restaurant on 145th Street) had opened an establishment on 125 th Street. The brunch meeting was held there.

As I entered and took my seat I surveyed my surroundings. Many influential Harlem pastors were present. Coach Bill McCartney, a college football coach of some fame addressed the gathering. Other Christian leaders of the city who sponsored the event accompanied him. When he finished speaking we were asked to share our thoughts. After a few remarks from those present I decided to contribute to the discussion. I spoke from my heart expressing both my reservations and the potential possibilities. My reservations outweighed the possibilities, but because of God it was necessary I show support for their expressed intent.

My reservations were based on their voiced concern for the unity and growth of all men in the Body of Christ. I know that White people have very little concern for the true advancement or improvement in the conditions of and quality of life of Black people collectively unless they receive the lion's share of any benefits accrued.

The potential, my understanding of God's desire for the unity of the Body of Christ across racial, ethnic and social economic boundaries, in spite of my natural misgivings. The possibility of working together in Christ to advance such a cause was worth the risk of an association with a White organization promoting their agenda. I sounded the gong.

I awaited the kiss of death. On the contrary I was embraced. I was approached at the end of the meeting by Richard Galloway and Andy Puleo. They asked for my name, church affiliation and phone number. They also gave me their contact information. They said they would be in touch. True to their word I was soon contacted and invited to attend a city wide strategy meeting comprised of Christian leaders from the 5 boroughs of New York.

Richard Galloway and his wife Dixie are the founders of New York City Relief. Their ministry dispatches a refurbished school bus into inner city neighborhoods of New York to provide food and referral services for those most in need. Together with Andy Puleo they initiated a task force to sponsor 'Wake-Up Calls' (rallies that brought awareness to men on upcoming Promise Keeper conventions). They were working out of the offices of the New York Bible Society with the cooperation of Chuck Rigby who directed the New York office.

Andy Puleo was a true Christ Ambassador. He is a Christian of Italian descent known by everyone. He was also quite comfortable getting to know anyone he didn't already know. He had the unusual ability to cross-racial, ethnic and denominational lines with ease. He was well respected and trusted across the various lines that divided us as a body of believers.

Andy was also an able street minister. He is at heart a street evangelist desiring to reach all people for Christ. He proved himself an able discipler as he embraced those in the Body and laid a firmer foundation for them to build on their faith in Christ. He showed no partiality to provide the same instruction for the less fortunate and newly saved. Andy is truly a man of honor and integrity. I bought into the possibilities that were laid before me on the strength of who he was. In doing so I recognized I was out of my league, not because I couldn't hang, but because I wanted my center to be in God. If I was going to be of benefit I needed the help of God.

In 1994 my maternal grandmother passed from this world. Mrs. Weldon Cunningham was a staunch believer in God from her youth and a well established member of Metropolitan Baptist church. I fully expected her funeral services to occur in the church she was so well known in. To my surprise I was asked to preside over her home going at my church.

Something was shifting in the spiritual realm. I was saddened over her passing, but honored at the request to preside over her funeral. My grandmother's home going drew all my family on my mother's side from far and near. God was about to do a new thing. He wanted all to see what he had done. I looked to the Lord for direction and He provided all I needed. Family and friends who I had not seen since I was a little boy were present. One such person was Florence Ann, my grandmother's goddaughter. I didn't know anyone was still in touch with her.

After the services she came up to me and said you are just like I remembered you to be. Through her words I realized a work of God had been completed in me. Gone was the evidence of the years I spent in drugs and crime. Revealed was the hope and promise people only see within one in childhood. Before I could adequately respond she was gone.

So many kind remarks were passed and shared between family and friends on that day that I longed to hear spoken. Even in passing my grandmother was able to rally her loved ones to a place of hope and joy while in the company of one another.

A new learning curve had begun.

At a meeting in the Christian Life Center, where Rev. Dr. A.R. Bernard was the Senior Pastor I worked with Andy and the committee to develop a plan of action for the burgeoning men's movement in our area. There were ten to twelve pastors present along with Dr. Bernard, Andy and myself. I was the only non-pastor present. I sensed an undercurrent. The title pastor was important in meetings with other pastors. Your influence is diminished if you do not pastor your own church. Knowing that, I comforted myself in the knowledge that I was invited and a part of the strategy committee.

As the discussion continued I was  somewhat perplexed. It appeared that the same workings were at play that I had experienced in prison, on the street and at community meetings.
Everybody seemed to be jockeying for position. Everyone had their own agenda. Many had no interest at all in providing ministry to men. Their concerns seemed to revolve around self interests. By all rights, leadership fell to Dr. Bernard whom I noticed was assured of this from the beginning. His heart truly revolved around ministry to men.

At one point during the discussion I asked, "I thought we were supposed to be men of God and not just men?" There was a slight pause, a few odd looks and the discussion continued. No one skipped a beat. Suffice it to say I grew to love and respect Dr. Bernard. It was a joy to be around him and see him work. I also grew closer to Andy Puleo who exposed me to this whole new level of ministry.

We gradually picked up momentum under Andy's direction and Dr Bernard's support. More and more leaders began to support the idea of hosting a Promise Keepers event in New York. And then we did it. In 1996 the Promise Keepers event took place at Shea Stadium in Queens N.Y. and I was an integral part of that accomplishment. Hopes ran high in New York as the reluctant and non-committed smelled success. Many jumped on the band wagon. Some came out of sincerity, others caught up in the tide and still others driven by selfish ambition.

Of the latter, one such character was Sheldon King. Sheldon was very intelligent. He was quick of mind and speech. A lack of self confidence was not his problem. He appeared out of nowhere. He made his presence felt and immediately began to press his agenda. After fleecing a few of their hard earned resources he absconded. He returned to the void from whence he came, never to be heard from again by any I know. I myself was disappointed finding out that the will of God was not always the upper most focus in the hearts of men named in Christ.

With success came more opportunities and more titles. We at the core became Gate Keepers of the city. I was invited to speak at different churches. My influence and recognition spread. I worked with local pastors to host the P.K. North East Regional Conference in Harlem. I was ably assisted by Paul Savage. Paul was a brilliant and gifted administrator. God performed a miraculous work in his life and it was a joy to work with him. My reflections on how God brought Paul through encourage me until this day.

In January of 1998 my mother passed after a year of illness. Three days after her passing my father-in-law, Richard Thomas senior passed. I asked God not to place more upon me than I could bear. Uncle Norris my father-in-laws brother, a pastor from Schenectady presided over the services and I lent ministerial support. It was amazing to recognize how all the parents of the children of my generation in my family struck relationships with God in their lives.

My mother's death drew both sides of the family together. Sometimes you can only fully appreciate the greatness of someone at the end of their lives. That was my experience with my mother. My mother was truly great. We speak of heaven often. We peer through life and draw expectations of who and what we will be in heaven. As a minister of the Gospel I have learned you can gauge the value of someone's life through the heartfelt movements of a home going service.

As I presided over my mother's service all questions concerning my station in Christ were finally put to rest amongst all my family. They came. They saw. They heard. Such an outpouring of God came forth as the members of my family clearly revealed the greatness of Mrs. Dorothy Cunningham-Spicer-Wilson, my mother. I know I shall see her again. It was my privilege to minister to my family and serve God who made it all possible. My mother brought me into this world and I was honored to escort her out.

I couldn't help reflect on the fact that all the parents of all the people closest to me had passed on and that I had become one of the family leaders for the present and coming generations.

I continued to work with other citywide and national ministries. I worked with Navigators, Concerts of Prayer with Mac Pier, Campus Crusade for Christ, Here's Life Inner City with Glen Klienkenect, N.Y. Bible Society, the American Bible Society, Dr. Paul DeVries and others. Slowly my confidence in what I was doing began to erode. I began to believe I could do more for Christ at Bethel than I was able to do spread out so far and beyond. I gradually began to withdraw so I could return my full attention to my first love, B.G.A.

The final straw took place in 202. A major meeting of Christian leaders was called. We met at the Christian Cultural Center, the new worship complex of Dr. A.R. Bernard. The building was breath taking and its vision all-encompassing. All the leaders were there. They stretched across all the arenas of our faith. With their presence came their agendas, but only Jesus Christ is Lord.

The purpose of the meeting was to adopt a strategy and appoint the leadership over a loose affiliation of Christian organizations and churches for our city wide Christian endeavors.

The strategy was laid out. Everyone was primed. The vote was taken and the Holy Spirit moved. But He did not move within the set agenda. When all was said and done a different strategy and leader was chosen. The opposition was disappointed and the unity God demanded foiled because some did not like the fact their desire was denied.

It was made clear. A lot of institutional Christianity is not about Christ. It is about maintaining position and power. It is about growth and advancement. It is about gifts and anointing. You will find the theme of money interlaced throughout. I believe God was grieved over what He had allowed me to see and understand.

The issue was racial. No one said it, but everyone knew it. It was a racial minority leader and agenda that was chosen. Several of our White brothers in Christ could not bring themselves to submit to that decision.

A true spiritual stronghold and a major area of deception the devil employs in the world is the presumption that might is right and to the victor goes the spoils. In America that dictum is reduced to – if it is white it is right. If you listen closely you can hear it whispered in the halls of power within the church. The truth is if it is God, it is, and must be, right. I believe the heart of God skipped a beat that day. It is so easy to miss God and believe you have not. The truth of the Christian faith is not of this world, though we have a need for the things in this world. Threading that distinction is where we are failing as the church. It is a difficult course to navigate.

This is not an indictment of White people. White people, as a collective, like all other people, are mostly under the influence of things that are not of God. We are all equally human; Blacks, Whites and all in between. The difference is Whites have predominance in the earth at this time. White nations have set the course for world affairs for the last 1,000 years. That places the focus on them because they exercise major power and influence over world events. The conditions that exist are primarily due to past decisions that White nations have made. (Might is right and to the victor go the spoils.) As the impact of those decisions trickle down, those on the bottom hold those on the top responsible for the frustrations and disappointments they encounter in life. Godliness is no discerner of persons. If an unforgiven wrong is committed, the seeds planted by those actions can and will produce corrupted fruit. It makes no difference whether an individual or a nation performs the deed.

Whether we are the oppressed or the oppressor we must acknowledge our wrong doings. Whether we are individuals or nations we must come to grips with the error of our ways. If I hurt you, your natural desire will be to hurt me in reprisal. The more we look to hurt one another, the more we will hurt one another for reprisal.

There is no righteousness in race, ethnicity or nationality. There is a racial responsibility, there is an ethnic responsibility and there is a national responsibility that we need to, but have failed to address. The failure of any group to live up to its responsibility does not relinquish another group from living up to their obligation to themselves.

African Americans must not adopt nor hide behind the failures of others. As painful as life sometimes is there is opportunity for improvement if it is sought. Righteousness is a quality of character. You must earn it. If you display unrighteous characteristics you are unrighteous. I have found I need an atmosphere of righteousness to sustain myself. Do you? It is God's desire to draw all into an atmosphere of righteousness.

I retreated to Bethel. Spiritually safe, I continued to grow and await God. Together with Rev. Gordon Williams we developed the community development corporation for the church. It was an adjunct formed to extend the possibilities available to us to further serve those within our community. Bethel continued to grow as the Bishop prepared to retire.

My final hurrah within this spiritual season was presented to me by my dear friend Andy Puleo. I was asked to speak at a national conference presented by the Navigators. Its theme was racial reconciliation. Earlier in the season I was invited to preach in a predominantly Chinese church on Central Park West. It was an honor and I was grateful for the opportunity. At the service I was accompanied by Praise Movement, a dance ministry led by Sister Joe Dell Hutcheson. I made every effort to honor God.

After the service I was approached by several of the members of the fellowship and its staff. They were moved by and pleased with the ministry presentation of dance and the word preached. In the excitement a question was raised. My response was I held back. In their mind I had pushed the envelope.

During the Navigators Conference the senior pastor of the Chinese church was one of the speakers of the day. He was not present at his church the Sunday I spoke at his church, but his staff who hosted me were present at the conference. The Spirit of God moved. I did not hold back. I said everything I believe God wanted me to say. After I shared a staff member of the Asian church who heard me speak at his church said, "I see you didn't hold back this time."

The institutional Christian community didn't believe God for what I believed Him for. If they did they were not willing to take it on. Maybe I was the problem or maybe what I believed was the problem. I decided to take both before the Lord for an answer.

I believe God demands more from us through faith than we are giving. The Bible surely states that He does. If He does demand more He will provide what is needed for us to accomplish His demands and we will have to surrender our resistance to God's love.

Bishop Ezra Nehemiah Williams
Pastor Emeritus of Bethel Gospel Assembly

My loving mother, Dorothy Spicer-Cunningham-Wilson

Top- Reverend Carlton Brown and his wife Lorna
Bottom- Pastor Carlton T. Brown, current Pastor          of Bethel Gospel Assembly

Staff of Beth-Hark Christian Counseling Center

300

Top- Tesha and Marcus      Middle- My son Walter III in the military
Bottom- Diane with Crystal and Felicia

Top- Walter III and wife Chiketta
Middle- Walter III's children, Renee and Tyra
Bottom- Family portrait

A man changed by God

303

Serving God and loving every moment of it!

# Chapter Eight

After the reconciliation between my wife and myself, I was a changed man. In our time apart I focused my attentions on the biblical truths of God, the wonder of spiritual reality and its influence and impact on the natural world. At the same time I paid a lot of attention to my self-development. I was turned inside out. My innermost self was exposed. I was redefined in relationship to the truth of spiritual reality expressing itself within me in the natural realm. Within that process my relationship to women as a man was explored and redefined.

As I grew in knowledge of myself I realized I truly like women. With the thought of sexuality removed, I am still attracted to women just because they are female. Sexuality was an added pleasure derived from the company you keep with them in matrimony. I found I liked their appearance, mannerisms and their state of being. Watching women move, talk and express themselves is a joy. It is not an obsession, but an appreciation. It goes beyond explanation. It is primal and innate. I decided I didn't need to understand it. All that I was required to do was to enjoy my appreciation of them.

After I gained control over my sexual desires during the lengthy period of my separation I would often long to have a woman of my own. As I was out and about I would see others together and question God. I would continually ask, "Why did I have to be alone?" I knew I could exist and do well without a woman at my side, but that made no difference. I wanted a mate.

My being ignorant, impatient and deprived clouded my heart and mind, perverting my sense of independence. I developed a warped sense of self-sufficiency. I was reduced to believing the only thing a woman could give me that I could not provide for myself was sex. Wrong! That misconception was at the core of my problem with women. To have a woman's sincere respect, concern and cooperation is self-gratifying and inspirational. It is my basic need. Buried deep under the disappointments of my life and within the innermost expanses of my heart I found this longing for those endearments from a woman in my life.

I understood women had their own point of view. They are different from men in more ways than we care to address today because of the idea of equality and political correctness. Considering this I realized the constructs of mankind cannot overshadow the nature of truth.

The relationship between men and women is complementary, compatible, even symbiotic. We are drawn to one another. We are the same, but different. They see, understand and express things differently. Their needs and expectations of their mates do not spring out of a male ethos, though our bond is seamless. One gender does not exist without total dependence on the other and through our union all humanity has come into being.

Being free of my own delusions, I saw that many of the issues I faced in my past were responses to what I perceived as faults in the character of the women in my life. If Diane and I were going to have an improved relationship I needed to be able to address those issues as they appeared. Her faults could no longer be easily concealed behind my blatant wrong doings, angry outbursts and negative attitudes. I knew what I wanted and I was better able to address those areas in her life that didn't tend to generate the respect, concern and cooperation I desired.

When my wife and I reconciled I thought she would return a better person for me. I thought she would have learned more from her experiences. She didn't. Diane had her own agenda expressed through her desires and ambitions. The reality for me was that to acquire the type of marriage I desired, I would have to work at it.

We were in the era when men were being advised to get in touch with their feminine side. What was believed then and is still believed today, is the problem of male communication. It is considered that men do not communicate with their wives enough. I would argue that men and women do not communicate the same. I will admit as a man I did not rely on oral communication as a means to express myself; especially if you are measuring my level of verbal communication against a female's. Sometimes it's just that women don't like the language a man uses and seeks to change a man into something he is not, namely comfortable being verbally expressive.

Nevertheless I realized greater communication was necessary if there was any hope of acquiring my idea of a healthy marriage. In my desire to do right I stretched myself to accommodate. I learned to articulate my feelings and observations with the help of God. I took the time to explain to my wife what I wanted and what was in my heart. She seemed to understand and agree with all I shared.

The relationship of marriage must function on three levels; the physical, emotional and the spiritual. In the physical realm is where most begin their interaction. I failed to explore my compatibility on the emotional and spiritual levels with a woman in the past. Emotional compatibility is more difficult to identify. Do you have the appropriate temperament? Do you have to make adjustments in your beliefs? Are you willing and capable of making those adjustments? The answers to these questions come in time and with effort. This process requires a degree of maturity and self control.

All these matters are made easier if you have spiritual compatibility. Spiritual compatibility goes beyond both of you being of the same faith. All who believe do not have the same calling in Christ. God has made all of us individuals. We look different. We have different physical features. We have different material needs. We have different personalities. We have different temperaments and emotional needs. We are called into different works. My refocus of these preconditions to my marriage helped bring about a healthy, seamless bond between my wife and I.

In my dealings with Diane I began to understand that a lot of her responses to me were not because of who I was or what I had done. Her attitudes and responses were derived from the multiple hurts and disappointments she had encountered with different men in her life.

The disappointments began with her father and older brother. More were added and the first ones continually reinforced as they trickled down and were evidenced within the various boyfriends she encountered before starting a relationship with me. I did not prove anything different to her in our initial involvement. It also did not help that the attitudes of most women she was exposed to constantly reinforced the negative experiences she encountered

I noted my wife had no place to retreat from the onslaught that assaulted her sensibilities. She had nowhere to turn to receive knowledgeable direction, communication or healing to allow her to develop a better understanding of her femininity, or a better understanding of masculinity. Through my limited experiences I believed women to be trustworthy and faithful if the men in their lives were meeting their needs. I concluded it was my responsibility to measure up as a husband. Hopefully my love and affection would be sufficient with the help of God to turn the tide.

It is necessary for two people to be in agreement to stay together. It is better if they share common desires. There are some basics to life that all people share, but beyond those basics are areas that can make or break a marriage. I have heard it said that it takes two to argue. My strategy was not to allow us to be drawn into contentions. The need was to address and solve differences.

A major theme of godliness is love. To be truly godly one must faithfully develop and integrate love throughout their lives. Many times I would find myself angry with my wife. With anger other feelings would be stirred in my heart against her. Outside of our home I had time to see to the needs of others as a display of the love in my heart. It took an effort to accomplish this because I did not always agree with some people in our discussions. The same could not be said in my marriage. At home I would entertain my frustrations. That was a major contradiction. If I allowed myself to continue in that way I would be a hypocrite. It was necessary for me to find a way to continually express my love for my wife even in adversity if I was worthy to be considered a godly man.

I worked hard not to be a hypocrite in my marriage. I concluded the best way to make a new start was not to make an issue of our time apart. Though I was curious about whom she was with, if anyone, and what was on her mind, I believed nothing good would come out of dredging through that period. I would forgive and not look back.

I made me the focus of my attention. I watched what I said and how I said it. I made sure I expressed my concerns without being overly critical, judgmental or projecting anger. I got better and better. I listened carefully to my wife. I began to communicate my thoughts and feelings so well my wife didn't want to communicate as much any more. She was clear on who I was, what I wanted and what I was trying to do.

Our relationship improved. I won my wife's respect, some cooperation, but not her concern. That I put in the hands of God. We worked well together financially. All household duties were not mandated around gender roles. We worked with what we were good at or best suited for. We both had a common desire to see the needs of children met. My wife continued her education and left her position in daycare to teach within the New York public school system.

312

We, being childless together, enforced the desire of my wife to adopt. I was more career oriented. I wanted a firmer financial foundation. As we discussed the matter I recognized her need to raise children went beyond reason. Reason is a wonderful tool to be used in life, but it is not always the best one to use. It wasn't a right or wrong discussion. In practical terms I was right and more reasonable, but to meet her need appeared more important.

Maybe satisfying this desire in my wife would generate the fulfillment of my needs. Providing for the unfortunate and raising children is an admirable quality in itself. As we ventured forth we found the process for adoption to be daunting. We were unable to find an agency willing or able to accommodate us. We were directed to foster care agencies. We were further led to understand we would have to become foster parents before we could adopt.

The idea of protecting helpless children is admirable. The idea of assisting those children to find stable homes and environments is also admirable. Like most things the process one endures to accomplish those goals is tedious and unpleasant to say the least. My past presented what appeared to be an insurmountable hurdle.

I was finding that it is harder to do right than it is to do wrong. Something always came up, something discouraging; something to hinder what I wanted to do. Something I never faced before. Something I had to figure out and face alone. It didn't make natural sense. It was always spiritual in nature. Forces contrary to God at work opposing what I was convinced I ought to be doing. It is a good thing to desire to strengthen your marriage. It is a good thing to open your lives to be a help unto others in need. Desiring these good things introduced a mental and emotional anguish that was unbearable. At those times I would commune with God for strength, guidance and reassurance.

Working with any bureaucracy can be frustrating. Each department refers you to a different department. You call to speak with someone and they place you on hold indefinitely. If you do speak to someone they give you inaccurate information and you have to start all over again. Working with the State agencies in the City only made matters worse.

Hoping to end our frustration my wife and I decided to go to Albany. Our hope was to expedite the matter by cutting through the red tape. At the time my wife's sister Sarah was living in Troy

New York. Troy borders Albany. Albany was smaller and we found it easier to navigate. We made one phone call and an appointment was scheduled for the next morning.

We made an appearance at the necessary office and were seen immediately. The staff was courteous and helpful. All our questions were clearly answered and we received accurate information on how to proceed. We scheduled a hearing to dispute what was on record regarding my past.

After appearing as witnesses and presenting our evidence at a hearing in New York City I was cleared to become a foster parent. The entire process took 2 years. The Albany visit brought closure to the matter in less than 3 months. What a difference.

My wife's desire was to parent an infant girl. As part of their policy we had to express that verbally and in writing. I don't think they were listening. After a bad experience and turning down several phone requests we received a call in 1996 to accept 2 sisters ages 3 and 4 into our home. I called my wife to give her the news and felt her excitement through the phone. My wife called Agency of Children's Services (ACS) to make final arrangements and schedule to pick up the children.

I still remember the first time I saw them. I was in Discipleship teaching a class with the residents. My wife walks in with the biggest smile on her face. She was so pleased. It was a Kodak moment, but I didn't have a camera. In either hand she had a little girl. The girls were quiet and wide eyed not sure of what was going on, but I knew we had the makings of a family.

Throughout it all the hand of God was moving. I cannot count the times He was available to confirm, assure, encourage, strengthen, direct, move an obstacle, present an idea, put words in our mouths, provide understanding, or remove anger, frustration or disappointment. God was parting the Red Sea to provide a home for Crystal and Felicia Barnwell using my wife and I as His agents. God is an awesome God.

The male female relationship is at the foundation of all human institutions. To ignore this is to scoff at the social cohesion necessary to keep a community of people together. These are high sounding ideas. In the past I flouted such considerations. My blatant disregard evidenced in the fruit of derision present in everyone's life around me. This derision appeared in the lives of the women I related to and the children bred on account of those relationships especially.

My reversion to sane sensibilities afforded correction that improved the well being of all my children. Each encounter with each child was handled differently, but for the same desired outcome. This time around I was given an opportunity to perform this parental obligation and responsibility in actual time. All the factors were present to complete the equation. There was the loving mother and father in marriage, faith in Christ and young children all living together under one roof. The practice of love on my part would be the bonding agent.

The focused and consistent caring, nurturing and provision of adults in a purified environment produced results. It could not be denied. It was working. The art of love had won the day. Crystal and Felicia flourished in our care. I saw their lives change for the better before my eyes because of what they received from my wife and me with the help of God.

God further provided the grace for my wife and me to form genuine relationships with the three older siblings of Crystal and Felicia. They are all wonderful children. It bears comment that the most difficult reach was the boys. The oldest boy in particular took the longest to come around. Though under all sorts of pressure not one of them is crushed, all of them are looking to a better future for themselves than the lives their parents presented to them.

Our assistance amongst these children allowed them brief opportunities to spend time together under the same roof under favorable conditions. This brought a joy to all of their hearts. It helped support their faith in adulthood and thus establish more faith in themselves. We went further and photographed the five of them together for the first time in their lives. My daughters treasure those photographs. They are prominently displayed in their bedrooms.

The three older children Joshua, Sean and Shauntay are Hallettes. They were fostered and ultimately adopted by Ms Bandy, a faithful woman of God. She was also the foster parent of the three older sibling's natural mother and father. Diane and I were not able to adopt Crystal and Felicia because they were returned to their mother.

In Christ I learned how to relate to my sensibilities. I feel everything. Sentiments felt and expressed in my youth threatened my social masculinity so they were suppressed to my hurt.

In Christ they were uncovered. Instead of hiding them I identified and interpreted them. I related to the discomfort usually experienced from them. In relating I refused to allow the discomfort to carry me into unwarranted places emotionally.

I felt hurt and rejection in my heart hearing the desires of Crystal and Felicia to return to their mother. My wife and I had provided years of love and support to them. How could they choose their mother over us? What made matters worse was our belief that their mother was not ready to meet the needs of her daughters. I reached a degree of maturity where all of this is being worked out internally. These are my inner thoughts and feelings. Outwardly only love and encouragement is expressed. I was accustomed to God communing with me in the recesses of my heart to give understanding and to ease disappointment.

God provided understanding concerning the bond between parents and children. There is a need in all children to establish that bond. There is also a destructive element present when that bond is threatened.  There is a healing that takes place in children's and parent's hearts when they are assisted and supported when attempting to secure that bond.

Felicia came back to us on her own. A few months later Crystal did as well without the help of children's services. It was after this experience that the relationship between the older boys and ourselves were strengthened. Since then the girls have maintained their relationship with their mother and father over the phone, by mail and occasional visits. I see their longing to maintain a connection with their natural parents and blood relatives. I see the hand of God in all these things.

God had proven Himself again. The male female relationship is the foundation of all humanity. A man operating in godliness is at the head of this relationship. All exposed to him will look to him for strength, support and example. The failure of men to rise to the occasion has brought about this dismal state of affairs we call life.

The influence of women in my life forced me to reflect more deeply into myself because of my desire and concern for them. Their subtlety and at times boldness in dealing with me forced me to consider other variations to express myself and rise to heightened and improved relational plateaus. I would not and could not have accomplished such a feat alone. It was not within me.

I believe power has been granted to men to heal the hurts of our women just as power has been granted to men to hurt them. It is easier to cause pain and destruction than it is to heal the pain and to rebuild what has been destroyed. The majority of the disappointments we receive from women is a direct result of the disappointments they receive from us. No man can take on the remedy to this on their own. It is a godly quest. The healing will only be provided through total reliance and trust in God by the man who has enough faith to pursue it.

 have seen great strides made in the healing of my wife. The total deliverance I desire has not been realized. I continue to hope in God that my faith in this cause will materialize. I look back over the twenty plus year journey I have been on with Christ and see all that has been accomplished. To it all I say thank you Lord for you are truly good and what you have done is marvelous in my sight.

# Chapter Nine

If I have learned or accomplished anything in my short life it goes without saying it has been with the help and examples supplied by others. In my pursuits I have met many along the way who have provided bearing for the course, pace and the ultimate destination I hoped to reach. My window into their lives provided a look at how I would like to be perceived and what qualities I needed to possess to possibly accomplish that perception. The finer qualities and characteristics I treasured in humanity were observed in all aspects and on all the levels I crossed in life. I found the negative qualities in all those stages as well. Sometimes I was able to perceive and understand them immediately and at other times I did not. When the appointed time of understanding would arrive I determined to internalize that knowledge.

The first person I recognize as influencing my life is Malcolm X. As far as I can remember I have always liked him. He was someone I admired from afar. It was during my incarceration at Clinton Correctional facility that I read his autobiography. I was able to identify with him completely. I was encouraged by his ability to rise above every obstacle life had set before him. I struggled with him as he pressed to improve his conditions. I rooted for him to beat the odds and to come out on top. I learned from him that I could accomplish whatever I set my mind and heart to. He honored me because he let me know I did not have to settle for what was being handed to me. I dishonored him because I chose to accomplish what I desired through crime. He represented my first image of all that a man could be.

The man who influenced me most in my life of crime as a dealer was Guy Fisher. Seeing him out there wheeling and dealing was an inspiration. Everything seemed possible. All you needed was the heart, strength and wherewithal for it to happen. He was young and brash. Fair play and respect seemed to be the traits necessary to succeed. Wealth was attainable if you could stay one step ahead of the blind lady with the scales. If you could move fast enough you would be all right. He never said any of this to me. All our conversations were business related for the most part. This is how I interpreted what I saw and experienced. His energy motivated me to go for broke and worry about the consequences later.

The two other men who influenced me in my life

of unrighteousness were Vincent, The Hunter, Williams and Robert, Walk a Mile, Yardley. Maybe they knew this or maybe they didn't. They did not look for recognition or appreciation from others. They did what they did and that was all that mattered. Both lived by principles that governed their personal lives. If you could live up to their standards you were okay. If not you needed to stay out of their way. Those principles garnered a respect for them from others and a confidence they realized in themselves. Both were self-assured.

Vincent knew whom he was and what he wanted to do. At the time I met him we both were in prison. His being in jail was of no concern to him. He knew he was going to be released and he waited with patience for the judicial system to see things his way. Ultimately they did. It was impossible to ignore Vincent's presence wherever he was. He understood the life he had chosen and expected everyone who chose to deal with him in that life to understand it as well. This understanding encompassed friends and foe. He was very intelligent. Vincent was not to be taken lightly. He was a man of few words. When he spoke he was straight and to the point. If you were wise you would take heed to what he had to say. If he were not clear on something he would ask. Once he was clear things were set. He didn't like, or keep company with, liars or phonies. I could see he was working things out in his mind as he quietly went about his business. Vincent was satisfied with who he was.

He was killed living the life he loved by someone who didn't understand the life he chose. In life he walked in the midst with others, yet when he walked he walked above them all.

Robert Miles, like Vincent, was a man to be considered. He did not walk in the midst of others. He stood above them. He was like a shadow. He would be there and you might not notice his presence. If he was there you can be assured he was aware of, and had an understanding of, everything going on in that space.

His self-assurance was not on display. His intelligence was portrayed as aloofness and taken as such by some. He knew others could not or would not understand the way he saw things. He was not intimidated by their misunderstandings, neither was he enticed to wallow with them in theirs. He was willing to share freely what he understood of life with those who showed promise and quick to dismiss you and your foolishness if it came to light. He understood the rules of life and demanded life pay him the respect due him. I am sure Robert is doing well wherever he is today if God has spared life.

Unlike Guy, Vincent and Robert were not so infamous. Yet both of them commanded the same degrees of success. They made millions and none were the wiser unless you were in the know. These guys were smooth. I liked them right off.

I tried to emulate the positive qualities of these three men as I pressed for success in the streets. Circumstance prevented me from joining Vincent or Robert in the streets but I longed for the opportunity to try my hand with either of them.

As my world began to implode and my dissatisfaction with my life in crime increased I longed for sense in the midst of the nonsense. In late 1981 Joseph Holland caught my attention. He was a middleclass blue blood. It was obvious in his bearing. Unlike others I encountered within the middleclass he expressed a concern for those less fortunate than himself in life. Lip service was better than nothing, but he didn't stop there. He took action. He refused his entitlement and social privilege to dwell in the midst of the less fortunate. His self sacrifice opened my heart to new possibilities and opened doors to better opportunities. I was no longer alone in my walk with God. There were others.

Joe did not stop there. He reached back into the world from whence he came and bade others to follow. He presented himself as a model. He cast a vision and provided leadership for those who joined him and thus increased the impact he made on those who needed help the most. Observing him apply self-discipline, determination and purpose lifted my hopes to new heights. His example of Christian manhood slackened the tension compressing my heart. God was moving beyond my narrow understanding of things.

The most profound influence in my life during that period was realized in the person of Sandy Van Dyk. She was kind, generous and without fear. Her sense of righteousness and justice exceeded my ideal. Her devotion and commitment to life, and to reveal truth, was genuine. She was a natural leader in female form. She was independent and self-assured without the arrogance and pride that usually accompanies the privileged. She shattered the racial barrier that separated my world from hers as if it was of no consequence.

Sandy was of Dutch ancestry living in Franklin

Lakes, New Jersey when we first met. She was married and considered herself a housewife. As she shared her experiences she would remark, just a few years ago I was happy at home baking brownies and cookies for my children.

She took my hand as an equal and led me into the world of the White middle class. She shielded me from their jaded thoughts and remarks and demanded they respect me as a human being. Those I met through her respected her wishes and accepted my presence in their world.

It was Sandy who introduced me to foreign missions. She sat on the board of African Inland Missions (A.I.M.). After leaving the organization she single handily birthed a mission effort in Kenya. I was privileged to go to Africa with her as she labored to give life to her project with the help of God.

Sandy understood the economic and political realities of life. She also acknowledged the ramifications bequeathed to indigenous Africans as a result of those realities. She took her faith in Christ and entered the battle on two fronts, the spiritual and the natural. She wanted to lead people to Christ and into economic self-sufficiency. She freely offered her time and resources to root a new reality in the lives of

328

those touched through her ministry and by her life.

At home she labored tirelessly to inform and motivate those in the Christian community of the need in Africa. They had a responsibility as Christians to be involved in foreign missions. She was not consumed by guilt or looking for thanks. Her motives were as pure as her heart. She was looking to empower the denied with the knowledge and help of God. She made it sound and look easy as she cloaked all of it within the realities of Christ. The remaining social concerns engulfing my heart dissolved. They were replaced with a new hope for life through the promises of God. Continued faith in God would win the day. I think fondly of her even now. Of all whom are no longer present in my daily life I miss her the most.

The greatest man in the institutional church to influence my life was Bishop Ezra Nehemiah Williams of Bethel Gospel Assembly. The organized church is not my favorite place, but if someone must be a part of an earthly institution it is the only one worth being a part of as things stand. Bishop Williams personifies the goodness of God in the institutional church. He understood the importance of material things, but always put people first. He understood the church was not made up of brick and mortar, but of people.

His ability to show and provide love to all was truly an example to aspire to. I learned to believe that each person has a contribution to make no matter how small. He took the time to grasp what God was doing in others. From his position he would encourage them to bring forth their offering. I bet you are thinking monetarily, wrong. His focus wasn't on money or personal ambition, but the nurturing of souls and improving the quality of life for others. He was the first man in the world of church I submitted to. It was under his leadership I was allowed to grow and mature as a man of God. He was patient and understanding as he worked with me and smoothed over my rough edges. He drew out my desire to serve and please God.

Possessing a humble spirit he welcomed me into his presence. His regard for a person revealed how important you were to him and to God. He made the work of God seem effortless. His joy in doing God's work was genuine. I am thankful I had the opportunity to observe and serve under his pastorate. I miss his leadership. Bishop Williams taught me how to truly love God, God's work and God's people.

Andy Puleo is the most down to earth man I know. Being fully aware he turns a blind eye to the racial and ethnic divide that brings discord into the church. He is a man who displays godly character. He freely moves throughout the Body of Christ identifying and associating himself with those who put the will and character of God first. He is valiant. He takes up causes for the advancement of the Kingdom of God before they become popular. He goes forth alone if need be to gather the information and resources necessary to inform those who are willing. He takes the time to nurture those slow to grasp and is patient with all. He relies completely on God.

Andy is a humble man and has enough ministerial and administrative gifts to attain higher ambitions. That is not his passion. In his pursuits his only desire is to fulfill the will of God in this life. His true ambition is to please God and to reap the reward the Lord has set aside for him in the life to come.

The Bible speaks of Christ's ambassadors. Of course all Saints acquire that title by faith. Andy has earned the title.

He is selfless; ministering both to needs of people and his family. He is someone of the few that I have met who has learned how to strike the

balance between family and ministry; a true
family man. His wife is content, his three sons
prosperous and God fearing, and he is at peace
with himself. There are no pretensions. With
Andy I learned you could have it all if you do it
God's way.

Reverend Doctor A.R. Bernard represents the
institutional church at its best. I know him
personally and have worked with him on a few
projects, but I am not on his level. Dr. Bernard
walks free of the restraints that bind and cripple
the average church institution. He rises above
them all and beckons them to follow.

At a conference he shared his testimony as a
pastor. In 12 years, from the time he planted his
first church of a handful of members, he has
provided pastoral leadership to multiple
thousands. I first encountered him when he was
Pastoring at the Christian Life Center in
Brooklyn. The fellowship was housed in a space
that was once a supermarket. The main
auditorium could seat around 800 individuals
and he oversaw 4 services each Sunday. His plan
for the Christian Cultural Center was already
underway.

The admiration and respect he garnered from his
peers was evident. In the meetings I attended he

arose above dispute. Those who disagree with his points of view do not challenge him to his face. He is calm, reserved and assured. He knows his business and has the faith and works to prove it. Anyone can talk, Dr. Bernard accomplishes.

The liberty he displays in the Spirit has been a breath of fresh air to me. To hear about him I would have thought his strength and discipline came by great effort. After observing and listening for myself I knew his strength was not found in himself. His strength was found in Him he trusts, namely Jesus Christ. Dr. Bernard epitomized what God can and will do in the life of someone who is totally committed to God.

Bible stories are fine. Many preach the accounts as past events. They are a great deal more than that. The stories in the Bible are the greatest evidence on earth to the wonders of God past, present and future. They are examples of what God can do and what He is able to do. With all my love for the written Word, it does my heart glad while increasing my hope in this life to know that Bible stories are not just Bible stories.

It is one thing for the child of God to understand the wonders of God in what they see; it is another thing altogether when people who do not reverence God stand in awe beholding the evidence of God's wonder in life. God is revealing the truth of the stories of the Bible through the ministry and life of Dr. Bernard for the entire world to see. In my eyes God has lifted him above the spiritual mundane and catapulted him into an arena where the voice of God must be seriously considered. If God is willing and my success assured, the work I plant would be watered with the wisdom God has afforded him.

There have been other luminaries in my life; each contributing their information at their appointed time. The ones I have mentioned are they who impressed me immediately and most deeply. This cloud of witnesses over my life was my signpost. They provided insight, hope and inspiration for my hungry soul. Without them I am assured I would be less than I am today and none closer to what I hope to be tomorrow.

## Sibling perspectives:

### Rebecca:

Walter you were bad. You started fires. Later you were not around. You were not trying to hang out with anybody.

### Betty:

Walter what do you want me to say? You played hooky from kindergarten.

## Keith:

Walter is my older brother. I can't say for sure what my earliest memories of him were. Maybe they're of when I started kindergarten. I think his first assignment with me was to take me to school. PS 157 was on Saint Nicholas Ave. and 127th Street. It was a bustling time. I strongly believe we used to walk to school together. I was under his tutelage. He had the makings of a natural born leader. I would like to say he led me straight to school and he had compassion. He sort of looked after me. I don't know if it was from our mothers edicts, his personal experience, or neither, but he looked out for me. When I began school Walter was in I'd say the 3rd grade. I was in kindergarten. I'm not sure how many grades ahead of me he really was but he was ahead of me in grades. I didn't really see him in school, but we would meet and go home together at the end of the day.

Walter loved to sing. I don't know if he could sing or not, but he used to sing all the time. We had a songbook. One of his favorite songs was 'Home on the Range'. Another favorite was 'The Daring Young Man on the Flying Trapeze'.

Walter was pretty active and aggressive. I don't know if it started in the first year I went to school or maybe when I was in the 3$^{rd}$ grade or so, but I started to recognize some things. We used to return after school to the school. Walter would be looking for something and I had to be with him. We were rummaging around the school. He would take me into classrooms after school looking for money. He took the candy money, the cookie money and the picture money if he could find it. It was during the time of the after school program. Walter didn't participate in that a lot. I think our mother told him to stay for the after school program.

Then there was some truancy Walter demonstrated. I didn't really feel it because I wasn't with him because he was cutting out. He had a truant problem. I didn't realize that then. By the time I got to 3$^{rd}$ grade, I noticed but in kindergarten, 1$^{st}$ grade and 2$^{nd}$ grade I didn't.

Walter was in smart classes. He was a very bright guy. I really didn't know it but he was in smarter classes than me. He always seemed to be happy.

So we grew up a little bit more and I guess I really thought I was rich. I thought I had everything I needed in life. I really didn't watch

TV a lot. Walter must of saw a little  TV. and understood a little more than me. He let me know that we didn't have anything. So we were looking, we were adventurous, craving. He demonstrated we had to go do this. I guess I was kind of with it because I knew Mommy wouldn't go for any of it, even a little bit. And I didn't tell.

In the 3 rd grade I began to grow. I began hearing more about my brother's experiences from others. He had friends, but I really didn't know any of his elementary school friends. The first friends I knew my brother had were from 277 and 127th Street area. We were under our grandmother's shadow. She lived in 277. We had a strong family back then and it was a very happy time for me. It was a very motivational time.

He had three good friends as far as I can say back then. I know he must have known other people but he had Butch Washington, Dallas and Al Hobson. We all did a whole lot of things together. We did a lot of things with people and particularly with our family, especially in the summer.

In the summertime we had fun. We would come out early in the morning. We couldn't come out too early because Ma would make us eat breakfast and do other things first. But when we

337

got out we had fun. We had a lot of fun in the winter too. When we had big snow or little snow we did snow things. We had snowball fights, built snowmen or tried to hitch rides on someone's sled. We did wonderful things. We used to slide down Dead Man's Hill in Saint Nicholas Park. We walked quite a bit back then too. But it was in the summer that we had the most fun.

We couldn't wait for the summer. We knew how good the summer could be. We knew there were a lot of mischievous things we could get into during the summer. People had larger families then; families with 5, 6 or more children in them were common. All the children in many of the families were one, two or three years apart. All the children were the same age as the other children in another family. They had a family member for each one of our family members. The adults were all having kids in succession and stuff.

Walt had all of his own friends, but he also hung out with me. I also had a friend that hung out with me. His name is Bernard. He was a member of the Degraffenreid family. We hung out a lot in the summer. He had an older brother the same age as Walt. There were a lot of them too. Walt didn't hang out with Sonny like I hung out with Bernard and Sonny didn't hang out with Bernard the way I hung with Walt. We kind of accepted that.

Walter was a leader. He kind of led us. He would watch out for my guys. Sometimes he would leave us. He would say, Keith go over there and wait; then he would leave. I guess he was going to hang out with his own friends.

We didn't have a bike. We didn't have a lot of store bought things, but we didn't lack anything. I knew we were poor, but it wasn't so bad. In our yearning for more we would spin tops and play with our bean shooters. We went swimming. We played tag, Ring-Ling Co-Co 1, 2, 3, Johnny on the Pony, dodge ball, baseball and softball. We ran races, jumped benches and flipped over the fences. We would always find something to do. Sometimes our parents would take us on picnics in the park; go to Bear Mountain or to Coney Island.

There were some groupings in the Saint Nick we did not hang out with. We didn't associate with the groups comprised of Tyrone Bodey, Rudy or Gregory Stokes, but I think Walt had a liking for them. They were the gangsters of the time. They would walk around in their big hats and bravado. I think they were interesting. I guess they were alright. I hardly ever saw any of them. They used to mess with people. We just steered away from them and came up with our own angles.

These were our yearning years. We started small. We didn't have any money to buy the little things we wanted like fish and chips. We hunted for bottles to get the deposit. We helped sell flowers. Walter started selling fire crackers. We would go to Spanish Harlem to buy fire crackers and return to the projects to sell them. We really wanted some fish and chips.

We did a lot on 125th Street. We would go to Daitch Shopwell and pack bags or maybe carry groceries for customers. We went window-shopping a lot. We never broke a window but we planned it. We stole glasscutters from Woolworths and W.T. Grants to see if we could cut through the windows. They didn't work. We opened cab doors in front of the Apollo to get a tip. We flew pigeons.

We had some accidents too. I broke my finger and Walter cut his foot real bad at the pool. He also stepped on a nail a couple of times and had to get tetanus shots. Meanwhile we were snatching fruit from Smiling Brothers, a fruit and vegetable store on 125th Street. We were hustling change at the penny arcade. When we would go to Colonial pool we couldn't afford to buy a doughnut on the way home. We would be so hungry. After arriving home we would have to sit there and wait for our food. Our mother would deliver some gravy and rice with liver, yuck. That was life in the early days.

As we got older and more proficient sometimes we wouldn't eat our mother's food. If we had to eat it we would wait until my mother wasn't looking; then we would throw our food out the window. That's why I kind of hated the high rises.

Through that period Walter was determined. It was like he was on a quest. He was after something. He wanted to be somebody and get something out of life. He never said that to me, but I could see it. Walter was bright. He wasn't athletic. He did not favor sports. He also didn't go around having fights. Walter knew a lot of people but he had a limited amount of friends. Most of the things we did together took place in the summer. This period covered about four years. In that time I did  everything Walter did.

Then things changed. He stopped doing stuff like that.  In the 3 $^{rd}$ grade I met Mark Stewart 'Stick-O-Lick'. Around the 5 $^{th}$ grade Mark started hanging out with Walter. Through Mark he met a group of friends from Lenox Ave. Walt had 2 sets of friends. One set from the projects and another from Lenox Ave. I had a group of friends. Walter didn't let all my friends hang out with his friends. Walter, Bernard and I with Dallas and Butch could hang out. Walter and Mark with Butch, Dallas and I, would never hang out.

Cecil was another one of my friends. We did some things with Cecil, but not much. Cecil used to run away from home. Because of him we knew there was calamity in the world. We found out a lot of people didn't live in a loving home and everybody didn't love their children.

Around this time our family was on welfare. We didn't like it. Mom would get the cart and go to collect the government food. We didn't want any part of it. Walter would cut out and be nowhere to be found. But we had to cut that cheese. I don't remember the peanut butter too much, but I remember us having cans of it in the kitchen cabinets. Mom used to make some dishes out of all that stuff. She would bake peanut butter cookies and stuff like that. She kept her house clean and she kept plenty of food there
As we got older we didn't want to eat the food Mom cooked. We preferred the precooked food from the store. It was always better. We wanted to eat Chinese food like shrimp fried rice or

meatballs and rice or macaroni. Those were
happy days.

In the 5<sup>th</sup> and 6<sup>th</sup> grade I had a better inkling of
what school was all about. I had a little more
maturity. I got to see Walter work a little more.
He was still doing some of the same things, but
he was cruising 125<sup>th</sup> Street more. We had a little
more freedom. It is still during the summer when
I am able to hang with him more. It was different
in the winter. I saw Walt every night when he
would come home, but I wasn't with him during
the day. We used to sleep three in a bed. We had
the boy's room and the girl's room.

Skateboards, maroon pants and steel toe boots
came out. We wanted them all. How to get them
was the question. We had great Christmases. Our
eyes would be shining. Walter had to have it.
Walter seemed to collect people. We all had our
assignments. Walter always worked with other
people. He would take advice and could be
influenced, but only if he thought it was good or
beneficial. Then he would come up with schemes
to get what we wanted. Walt had to be sly. We
would snatch Casualiers (a stylish hat of the
day). We would go to the Manhattanville and the
Grant projects and steal skateboards. We
snatched goods out of stores and ran. We took the

money we made and bought the things we wanted. We gave parties at Mark's house with the stuff we stole from the supermarket. We built the pigeon coop on the roof of Mark's building and the J.B. era emerged.

J.B. (John Brown) owned a candy store on 7th Ave. (called J.B.'s) where the teenagers were allowed to hang out. The Lenox Ave crew also used to frequent J.B.'s. These were the guys Mark introduced Walter to. Ceaser, the Darby's (James and Buster), Lawrence, Robert, Erskin and Lil' Clifford were all out of 127th Street and Lenox. Walter fell right in with them. Walter captivated these guys. He had ideas. He made plans about how they could do the things they wanted to do.

These guys were different. It is hard to explain. I'll just say they were not from the projects. Those guys were together, but they were hungrier than us. They were more aggressive too. Those guys were down for anything. After Walt started hanging out with those guys he stopped coming home on time. We used to have to be home when the lights came on. Walter wasn't coming home. Walt was about 14.

There were a lot of those guys and Walt was in the midst of all of them. Those guys had

344

forethought. Walter was hanging out with all these guys his own age, but they all had younger brothers my age. It was perfect. There must have been about 40 of them. But all 40 of us never were able to hang out together at the same time. Everybody in the group wasn't aggressive, but things started happening and I lost track of my brother. I started playing basketball and hanging out with my guys. Sometimes we would come together at J.B.'s and hang out together on 7$^{th}$ Ave.

One time we found a knife. We hid it in a drain near a church on 7$^{th}$ Ave. 20 years I checked that drain and the knife was still there.

In the projects our focus shifted from the 127$^{th}$ Street side. We started hanging out around 240 and 2406. These were buildings on 129$^{th}$ Street in the middle of the projects. I hooked up with Michael (Weedie). He was a Burgess. Walter didn't hang out much with the Burgess', though Weedie had a brother Walter's age. Weedie mostly hung out with Walter. We went ice-skating in Central Park. We used to walk all through that park shooting our bow and arrows. Then we started gambling.

That's when Walter really started to come out. That's when it became clear to me my brother was a leader. He wanted to win all the time. He always had to have the bank. He tried to skew the odds in his favor. He also could be charming. He was particularly charming when he was losing. If he was losing he would start negotiating. He wanted to know how much money everyone was going to give him back so he could play again and try to win. That's how we started giving a little money back to the people who lost. My brother would try to keep playing until he won. That's when Walter became a role model and people began to imitate his leadership.

Around this time we became the center of attention and other guys from around the projects would come over to gamble with us. Lonnie Ramson out of 225 with Matthew and Monroe Singletary (the twins), Lil' 'D', Bocott from 2410 (He was a 5 Percenter.), Donald Jones and his brother Eddie out of 237 and others. If Walter won all the money he would only give me a quarter. I would complain that's all and Walter would say, you only started with 15 cents. It did bother me, but I believe it helped me to build my character. Everybody used to go around saying Walter did this and Walt showed us that and Walt's going to do that all the time. Walter wasn't older than 14 or 15 at the time.

346

Walter was in his twilight at 14 or 15. He really made a switch around then. We were gambling all over the place. We gambled in all the buildings. We brought dice into the St. Nick. Big George the Housing Authority cop would chase us up and down the stairs. We weren't drinking, smoking or nothing.

Nobody was gambling and shooting dice in the projects before us. People started coming into the projects to gamble with us in the hallways and under the street lamps. People like Tank and New York Slim. These guys were real gamblers off the avenue. These were men who lived off the street. Walter couldn't do to them what he did to us. Walter was out of his league. These guys were in a league all their own.

Our games also brought out the real thieves and stick-up kids. Guys like LaBrew and Fred Black would come around. Walter got into beefs with these guys over money sometimes. He wouldn't fight, but he wouldn't let them push him around.

Walter at times would go off with another set of friends. He had some privileges I didn't have. I don't know where he got them from, but I didn't have them. Walt would send me upstairs and off he would go. Next thing I know he was at the Mance's house and had a relationship with

Stephanie Mance. I don't know how he got there. I was still beating girls up. Walter used to hang around a lot of girls, Linda Washington, Karen and Sharon. I used to think there was some hanky panky going on behind my back.

The next thing I know drugs came. Walt lost some of his energy. He started using drugs and hanging out with James 'Chuck' and Ray 'Fats' McNealy and Donald Jones. Chuck told me one day, Keith don't worry about Walter, he is definitely going to get some money so he can get high.

Walter wouldn't let me hang out with him in those days. He would say I am going to get something and leave me. I guess Walt was trying to hide what he was doing from the people that cared about him, but he was caught exposed. I never understood it. I didn't figure it out and I didn't want to. Even with that my brother wasn't like a lot of the other fiends we grew up with. They would get high and be nodding all over the place. Not Walter. He went all out and all the way. Walter learned from that experience. Everything he did was grandiose. Walter didn't have a lot of shame about him and took pride in everything he did. Walter even excelled as a dope fiend.

Walter's whole mood had changed. People were telling me that my brother was out there committing major crimes. I remember thinking my brother grew up. I wanted to stay a kid, myself. I didn't know all of the details, but he was still just as determined as ever. I lost track of him again. Walt was off my radar. The only way I caught up with him then was when he came home from time to time.

Things really got heated when he came home that way. When he did come home he would steal something. If someone asked him about something that was missing he would lie through his teeth. He knew he took it. They knew he took it. I knew he took it, but he would never admit it. He was breaking my heart. It was clear to me Walter had a problem. My seeing him in that condition helped me to make better decisions for myself.

After that my brother went to jail. He was around 16 or 17 I think. His going to jail hurt me too. People around me used to say your brother is in jail. A lot of people badmouthed him while he was away. I didn't know how to deal with that. Nobody put their hands on me, but they were always saying things. At the time, someone going to jail was a novelty. Walter was the first one in our set to go to jail. I think I was in the 8<sup>th</sup> grade I started to smoke reefer and stuff like that. While he was away I did not go to visit him. I think I might have written a letter or two.

That's when I changed. I moved all around the projects. I shifted to 217 on 7<sup>th</sup> Ave. This is another area of the projects. Walt came home and found out I was smoking reefer. He came to me and said I heard you are smoking reefer. That's as far as you go. I am not going to let you go any farther. I am looking at him. I am thinking I can't be like him. It wasn't said, but I knew my brother didn't want me doing the things he was doing.

When I was in high school and things picked up Walter was doing a caper here and a caper there. I can't say when, but he came home and some of the guys were making money selling drugs in the projects. Just like that Walter kicked his habit and all of a sudden he started selling drugs. Walter had changed again.

Now Walter was going all out selling dope. Walter was bold. He was willing to take a lot of risks. Walter found out other eyes were watching while he was peddling his merchandise and he goes back to jail for him that was like a bump in the road. Every time he came out there was more and more money to be made in the drug game.

Walter would come home and tell me all the things he learned while he was away. He takes us out to Queens to connect with guys he met while he was away. Walt came home. He jumps in and he made the money. You could see it on him. We were going to be rich.

My brother was generous, not overly, but generous. Walter's giving me money staid my ambitions to sell drugs, but if everybody started buying cars no way I wasn't going to buy me a car too. We bought cars, medallions and anything else our hearts desired. I don't remember my brother being an excessive gambler, but he spent a lot of his money on clothes, getting high and other stuff.

Walter hooked up with Myrna when he was running with Dudley Payne. Myrna taught Walter a few more tricks and Walter ran with them. Indian and L.A. were on the set. These were the Guy Fisher days. I couldn't say much to my brother then. I was just getting out of high school. Walter was still the man. Never through any of these eras did his confidence in himself fail.

Walter's ideology has always been, if he wants something he is going to do whatever he has to do to get it. What I didn't understand is why he didn't delegate others to do things for him. That confused me. Walter would always do things for himself. The thing about my brother is that he didn't just talk about doing something, he really would do it.

The last time my brother went to jail people said by the time he came out everybody would be rich. It will be too late for your brother. Then he came out. He came back different. Walt was more aggressive and assertive. Maybe he was tired. People were gone. Some were dead and others in jail. The scene was a little different. All the guys from the 131st Street side of the Saint Nick were out there. The guys off the hill were out there and the money was drying up. Walter did a few things with the younger guys we grew up with and he made sure he got a share of the proceeds. He met Diane and kept on going.

My brother was a role model, but I had to stay away because he was too bold. Walter provided me an experience to judge my own actions by. I took a slower path. I was glad he allowed me to hang out with him. A lot of people's lives were destroyed selling drugs. They took advantage of other people or messed up people's money. Walter wasn't like that. He didn't get hurt by anybody and he didn't go around hurting anybody as far as I am concerned.

After a time I began to worry about my brother. He was deep into the dope game. Then he got religion. He changed as dramatically as he had changed before. He quit hustling and I didn't have to worry about him any more.

## Darryl:

I am Walter's youngest brother. I was not around him very much as we grew up. My older brother was never there, but he was there. We had a nice family situation. We had our squabbles, but everything was fine. I know I loved him and he always loved me. Coming from the family we came from we always had that love and we still do.

I was the outdoors athletic type. I directed my energy into sports. Walter was different. He wasn't a big television watcher. He didn't have an athletic body. He could swim very well, but he didn't have a real interest in sports. He just had a lot of energy. He had a lot of mental energy. Walter liked being out doors. He always seemed to be into something. He was always on the go.

When we used to go to church we would have to walk. Walter and my other older brother, Keith would go jingling in the phone booths. Once we got to church, which was across 110th Street (the church was on 108th Street) they would tell me to go into the church and they would go across the street into Central Park for adventure. That was Walter. The best way I can say it is that Walter is an adventurous kind of guy.

He seemed to always have something on his mind. He was always into something. He had ideas. Not only would he formulate those ideas, he goes and attempts them. He had no fear of attempting what he had on his mind. The majority of the time he achieves what he goes after. Sometimes I had a hard time looking up to this guy. He was always doing something, good or bad, he is doing something. His time is never wasted. He has get-up and go. He believes there are things to be done. There is a big world out there. That is why I am never surprised when I hear Walter did this. Walter did that. Walter is involved in this. Walter is involved in that. Walter had vision.

When he was little we used to call him Bug. He stopped us from calling him that. I remember he fell and busted his head open in the house and the time we went swimming in Colonial Park pool and he cut his big toe very badly.

He was never involved to my knowledge and I don't recall him being into a committee like thing. He was more independent. He always had friends and he did things with others, but he wasn't committed to any one person or group.

Walter had multiple talents. He could draw. He built model cars, planes and ships. Our mother kept a model ship he built in the living room for years. When he was in the Boy Scouts I used to go down and look through the window. They had snakes and stuff like that in there. He taught me the basic moves for chess. He played Loadies and took me squirrel hunting in Central Park. I know he used to steal bikes and reassemble them in the hallway on the 5th floor. I saw him get into a couple of fights.

I saw his drug paraphernalia lying around when he was shooting heroine. It was crazy. Ma was always at him during that time. During the riots and the blackouts I stayed close to home. Walter didn't. Like wow, he was in the midst of everything. Walter ran into Diane during the blackout of 1977. He took her as a good luck charm. Diane was a friend of my younger sister Felecia and her older brother Ricky was a friend of mine.

I remember a time I went down South. When I return I hear from some of my buddies. They are telling me your brother is into this and your brother is into that. They tell me my brother is involved in drug selling. Why don't you get involved? He's the one to see. I am not saying he ever tried to entice me or anything of that nature, but I do remember the time he robbed the ice cream truck in the dead end on 129$^{th}$ Street

I went to visit my brother one time in prison. He could only have one visitor at a time. Walter arranged for several of us to come at the same time to visit different inmates he had selected. After getting in he came and talked to everybody that was there to see him.

Sometimes people are very insensitive and cruel. They say and do many things that can hurt you. A lot of people had a lot to say both good and bad about my brother. Walter recognized that, but he didn't seem to pay any of them any mind. He just did his thing and moved on.

Walter was not the average big brother type if there is such a thing. He was always there for me if I asked him for anything, when I could catch him. At times when I ran across his path he didn't use a lot of words like a lecture. He would say stuff like, "Stay in school. Don't be a fool." Or, "Don't play yourself cheap."

Walter was not a bad influence. He never misled anyone. As a matter of fact he was an encouragement. He was a very encouraging kind of guy. He is a caring individual. He cared for people. I used to think nobody was around me for me. Everybody seemed to know and talk about my brothers. When my mother used to send me to J.B.'s to buy ice cream (that was Walter's hang out) Ronald "Abeka" Nesbit used to call me Lil' Walt. I don't know everything my brother Walter was into, but I was recognized as being Walter's younger brother.

Me myself, I am still growing today. I guess Walter was grown at birth. He had a lot of energy then and he still has a lot of energy now.

## Felecia:

There have been (and continue to be) several stages in my life with my brother Walter (I have always called him Walt [pronounced "Wort"]). From my point of view, in the earliest years he just started out being my big brother. As my formative years progressed he seemed unfamiliar to me. During my pre-teens, I became fearful of him. In my teens, I found Walt's generosity to be

357

abundant. I eventually found him to be responsive regarding my stated needs. By my late teens we were beginning to get acquainted. During my early twenties (the 1980s), as I engaged more with him, my admiration grew for him. He and I became really close during the 1990s, and by the year 2000 (in my forties) he declared he counted me as a friend.

In my beginning, there was not a lot of interaction between Walt and me (being nine years his junior). I was approximately 8 years old when I really became regularly conscious of him, and conscientious about myself around him. For me, home consisted of Mommy, Darryl, Keith, and Betty. Both Walter and Rebecca (we call her by her middle name, Jean) did not interact with me, nor were they inside the house, on any consistent basis, during the waking hours. So, life with Walter materialized for me in my pre-teens.

My early (age 10-13) impressions are that he was very generous, always giving; yet, he was scary, because he would leave hypodermic needles in plain sight on the bureau or an open top drawer, along with wads of money. For some reason, I had already developed a morbid fear of needles. Moreover, I would occasionally witness my brother deep into a dope fiend's nod (with a sluggish facial expression and ashy skin). Those images were a stark contrast to my dainty sensibilities. Years later, Walt's image changed, and the memories of him around the house were: his coming to visit our mother, presenting her large bouquets of red roses, giving her huge sentimental greeting cards, wearing stylish suits, with a matching wide brimmed hat. His greeting me always meant he would pull out a huge wad of money and peel off some dollars to hand to me.

Outside of the Wilson household, I noticed that Walt garnished a lot of respect (street credo, as they say). Although, the full nature and gravity of his activities were foreign to me, the benefits of his reputation became clear quickly. My having a big brother with street credo turned out to be a huge asset for me. (And for some of my girlfriends who didn't have older brothers). I extended the cover of protection I received to sometimes protect others. Although Walt was usually in the presence of young men society would consider being "bad boys", his associates were always very nice to me. Many years passed before I understood that these relationships were dangerous. My brother Walt, and several of his cohorts were my omnipresent protectors around the neighborhood.

For many years, because of his associations, I received many gifts of "boosted" merchandise from Walt. I was the envy of many. Through, and by, Walt's street reputation, I grew up in a tough environment, never fully realizing the graveness of the situations. It is my belief that Walter consequentially absorbed and diverted most of the world's danger away from me. I took my "hit" from living in "the projects, the ghetto, the hood, whatever", but the devastation that befell so many around me, seemed to avoid me, Thank God. On one hand, I believe my care came from God's grace bought and paid for by our mother's prayers, but in the flesh (or the other hand); my brother Walter's street presence kept the vipers away from his little sister. Some kind of street rules or unwritten honor code, or just good fortune, who knows?

It was not until Walter was imprisoned that I got to know anything about him, from him. He was, as one would expect, very responsive to my letters while he was in prison. For the most part, he was getting to experience my early growth and development, but what seems to have happened is, seeds were being planted for an extremely long journey we were about to embark on, unbeknownst to me or him. By the time he came

360

home, our lives were less divergent in some ways. I would see him more, because he tended to interact with our brothers more, and Darryl and I already had overlapping, interconnected friendships. I was approximately fifteen and becoming a bit of a handful myself, but I could always count on Walter; he always stood up for me. Whenever I cried out, he provided what I deemed the appropriate response. Sometimes I just wanted some guy I didn't like or care for, to leave me alone. Occasionally, it was some neighborhood bully, with a thug mentality, who didn't realize I was Walter's sister, who needed talking to. For instance, one time this other guy with street credo, named Brody, took offense to my outgoing nature while we were playing a game at a local pool hall. Without so much as a word, he pushed me and I stumbled and fell. A girlfriend, Diane (who took me to the place), and several younger girls from the neighborhood were there (and laughing). I was so embarrassed. I knew I would hate Brody forever, and I did. However, the afternoon of the next day, while I was just walking about my business, Brody approached me and apologized. He said, "I didn't know you were Walter's sister." I didn't even have the chance, that time, to tell Walter that Brody had offended me. I later learned that our brother Darryl had confronted Brody. It was widely known among dealers that Darryl was Walt's brother. Brody must not have wanted to experience any confrontation with Walter, so he quickly apologized to me. It sure wasn't out of any respect for me, because the night before he was sure-footed while both attacking me and relished antagonizing me until I left the building humiliated and totally pissed, feeling powerless.

Society-at-large, via it laws, placed no good value on the things Walt had been doing, or on his existence. Our sister Betty, the self-appointed moral judge and jury of the family, made her negative opinions known on occasion, but as for me, Walter was the only person in our immediate family who never made me feel bad about being me. In all of his corruption and rule breaking (determined by his frequent incarcerations), Walt's deeds, actions, and reputation placed an invisible shield around me and kept me from harm.

I was the lamb who survived the jungle. Living like it was paradise, because my big brother was the storm that went before me and cleared a path of less harm and resistance for me. Because of him, I never used hard drugs, I never dated any drug dealers, and the thugs, punks, riffraff, and gangsters of the community never harmed me. His lifestyle gave my life a chance. Even though he never really paid much attention to me, I paid attention to him.

## Chapter Ten

The Bible proclaims the history of existence from Genesis to Revelation. The book of Genesis outlines the beginning of all things and the book of Revelation is the prophetic voice of God foretelling what we would call the end of time. Sandwiched between these two books are the presence and movements of God in the midst of mankind throughout the earth. The Spirit of God is moving. King David asks, "where can I go to hide from thy Spirit Lord?" It is impossible to escape the presence of God. Jesus says the moving of God's Spirit is like the blowing of the wind. Like God the wind comes and Goes as it pleases. The wind's movements do not require man's permission and neither does the movements of God.

In the New Testament it is said, "In Him we move and breathe and has our being." God's Spirit moves blithely through time and space bringing to pass all that God has foretold in its season. One's denial of God does not render Him none existent; it only blinds them in His presence and to His movements. Humanity prefers to render what is seen to natural phenomenon.

The Holy Spirit of God is the most misunderstood and contentious subject amongst those who profess to be Christians. Each denomination, faction and persuasion has their own doctrine governing the reality of God's Spirit. I do not purport to be theologically astute or knowledgeable to break down the arguments amongst the various persuasions, but I do believe in the power and presence of the Holy Spirit. I have reasoned that it is not my place to qualify that, which is qualifying me.

When I was younger I would see people in church fall under the influence of the Holy Spirit. During those times some would scream, holler, jump, stomp or dance. Music would be played in accompaniment stirring the fervor and exciting even more those moved by the Spirit. Some people would fall out in what appeared to be exhaustion. I avoided and later denounced such behaviors because they were too far a field of the ordinary. I do not doubt the Spirit of God surely moves in that capacity, but I am sure God does not limit His presence or verification of His power to those few in the church who fall under His influence in such obvious demonstrations.

As the Lord was drawing me nearer to Him (By His Spirit) I often wondered who or what I was dealing with. I believe angels handled many of my experiences, especially in the earlier days. There is no way I can prove this. It is just a feeling I have. It is a sense of awareness. As I grew and yielded to what was drawing me those feelings began to sharpen. I became aware of God's presence. It was through my belief that God was real that my sense of His presence increased. I know the proofs of science have been elevated to the heights of undeniable truth. I believe in science and it has its place, but I also believe in something more. I believe in that certain unexplainable thing that seems too often occurs within life. I believe in that thing that must occur in everyone's life that science has yet to conquer. I believe we are something more than science has defined us to be. I believe in something I cannot fully explain.

After overcoming my distrust of allowing something I could not see or was not sure I could control to influence me I surrendered to the Word of God and the urging of the saints regarding the Holy Spirit. My first encounter was bazaar. It was definitely out of the ordinary. It was akin to an out of body experience. The more I surrendered, the more I observed myself from beyond. I was separated from myself yet still very much connected. I was me watching me as if I weren't myself. I observed me make all sorts of grunts and growls. My body resisted. I continued to release myself as I watched from afar. After a period of time I spoke in tongues and my body convulsed. It was like a burden being lifted from over my life. I experienced a relief and a comfort all at once. I was baptized with the Holy Spirit.

There were still many areas within me that were not surrendered to the presence of the Spirit of God. There were things that I desired to do that did not agree with what I should do as a man of God. As each domain in my being was subdued greater awareness of the presence and reality of God emerged. The point of view I held in the past on life broadened. My understanding of things increased and took on broader dimensions. It expanded beyond my self-centered view of life and the world. My conscious mind merged with the awareness of the presence of God. This included the understanding that God is here and has always been here doing what He said would be done. Before Christ I could not see God because I was blind. I could not see Him because I could not see anything that was not accepting of what I thought was important.

To understand more of the Spirit of God I had to

believe in the Spirit of God. It was the Spirit of God that led me to Christ. It was the Spirit of God through Christ that led me to believe in God. It was the Spirit of God through Christ and God that led me to believe in the Holy Spirit. I began to understand that it was the Spirit of God that had been at work in my life all my life. It was the Spirit of God at work in all things relevant to life. Things I took for coincidence or good fortune were not. They were steps God was taking or pieces of a puzzle God was placing together in my life to draw my attention to Him. They were measures God was taking to evidence His reality in life.

This was not an isolated experience specially designed by God for me. This phenomenon is a constant occurrence that takes place in the life of every living human being daily. As areas within my being were restrained it became apparent that the Spirit of God is always moving, was always moving and will always be moving. In Him we move and breathe and have our being. I became aware of the fact that the Spirit of God is moving throughout the earth and beyond.

I have a natural propensity to deny the existent reality of God. This inclination exists in all mankind in varying degrees. My denial and ignorance of God did not render Him nonexistent nor make Him ignorant of me. Humanity's misunderstanding and perversion of God's reality does not render God null and void in the affairs of His creation. God says that He will do nothing until He first informs His prophets, and that is just what He is doing.

As my understanding of these thoughts developed I would at times fall under the influence of the Holy Ghost. Usually it is not with a jump and a shout accompanied by music. It usually occurs when I am meditating or reflecting on the goodness of God. At other times it occurs when I reflect on the happenings of my life or when I am trying to express to someone what I hope to receive from God in life. Sometimes when the Spirit moves I am swallowed in emotion and overwhelmed with tears. Other times my heart is so filled I fold in awe and wonder as I muse over the goodness and mercies of God.

Without the presence of the Spirit of God a church is nothing more than an empty shell. It is dead if it lacks the presence of God. Churches are born, grow, live and die just as people and everything else does in life. The Apostolic, Pentecostal, Charismatic and Holiness movement concentrated its focus in God on the move of the Spirit of God. Sensationalism reigned during the earlier periods of the movement.

As the churches and the movement matured as in Bethel only remnants of the early emphasis persists. Most times the Spirit just fills the house or there is a prophetic presence in the sanctuary ready to erupt. Tourists visit the church on Sundays to take part in that experience with us. They are excited by our vitality and expressed devotion to God. Sometimes the Spirit is so thick in Bethel you can literally feel Him engulfing the entire congregation. What to do with Him is the unasked question.

Different churches acknowledge the moving of God's Spirit differently. Yet there appears to be a common thread. The Spirit of God is always resigned to move in the context of that particular church. The prophetic word to individuals is always positive. It is never dramatic. The prophetic word concerning the world is always negative. When something negative is prophesied it is usually so generally stated it could apply to anyone. Sometimes the words spoken over ones life doesn't come to pass. If a prophetic word is ever brought to question, the blame always falls on the failures of the saint and not the failure of the prophet.

When the Holy Ghost moves in the house of God

people are immediately impacted. Too often very little permanently changes for a person in their everyday lives. This could be due to either a lack of faith and obedience on behalf of the believer or a lack of power on the Spirit of God's part. I tend to believe it to be the former, but either way it is bad news for the church. The truth of our faith always stands as a witness of our faith.

The Spirit of God is an agent of change. Change occurs in the lives of those whom the Spirit touches. I would dare reason that the scriptures apply to the Spirit of God, as well when it says whatever you touch shall prosper. Shouldn't a touch by the Spirit of God produce evidence of that touch? Isn't God concerned about His power being expressed beyond the church? Doesn't the Word of God imply that at a minimum? The failure of God's power expressed within the four walls of the church has direct implications on the power of God moving outside of the church. Jesus could only perform a few miracles in certain locations because the people did not believe He could. They were of little faith. Acts 1:8 states that when the Holy Spirit comes you will have power. This lack of faith is saddening the heart of God and discouraging the unbeliever.

The Spirit of God is power. He releases His power

through individuals according to His will. It is
the believer who must first believe that God will
do what He says before those who do not dare to
believe. It is the will of God that mankind is
healed. God will perform miraculous medical
healings (external), but He is more concerned
with miraculous spiritual healings (internal). The
focus amongst the saints is to evoke the medical
healings (external). This misses the desire of God
entirely. At the other extreme some have given
up on the power of God to perform miracles so
they deny the power of God. In the middle are the
saints who faithfully watch and patiently wait.

More often than not the will of God is clear. He is
in the business of reconciliation. He is reconciling
man to Him. As His Spirit moves God is
reconciling mankind to Himself and mankind to
itself. He wants to restore marriage. He wants to
restore family. He wants to restore mothers and
fathers to their children. He wants to restore
children to their parents. He wants to restore
man to woman and woman to man. He wants to
restore the races and ethnicities to one another
and take the whole caboodle and restore it to
Him. You might not want that, but God surely
does. That is the purpose of the moving of God's
Holy Spirit throughout the earth.

The Holy Spirit took control in all these areas of
my life. The Spirit continually reminded me to
love my wife. He reminded me of God's mercies
and forgiveness towards me. I was encouraged
not to harden my heart, that it wasn't about me. I
was encouraged to forgive and be merciful. I was
asked where God was in what I was thinking or
feeling. Where was God in what I had a desire to
do? I was told to calm down and take it easy. I
was advised to think it through. I received a
sense of peace. I was asked what did I think or
hope to accomplish if I did this or said that. The
Holy Spirit was present long after the Sunday
shout was over reminding me that I was a child
of God and I must reflect who God is through my
life in everything I thought, said or did.

It was important to God that I be a good father to
my children. The Spirit of God came against all
my apprehensions. He encouraged me in my
times of frustration. He taught me to understand
that everything would be all right if I believe and
press forward in love. I saw Him at work
operating on my hardened heart and replacing it
with a heart of flesh. I became less selfish and
less self-centered. He sensitized me to the needs
of my children and helped me to recognize the
benefits they would receive in life if I cared for

them consistently. It was the Spirit of God that convinced me that my children were my responsibility.

God is love. The first characteristic listed in the fruit of the Spirit is love. True love is selfless. It exposed my faults. My feelings and intentions were laid out before me. I was afraid to express true love and it was apparent. The love of God contested the spirit of fear within me. I have heard insanity defined as someone doing the same thing over and over again and expecting different results. I didn't imagine myself to be insane. The only option available to me if I wanted life to improve was to take the risk and try love. I placed the interest of God and others before my own. The Spirit guided.

The Spirit of God taught me the power of love. He impressed love upon me after my salvation when I returned to my mother's home the first time. He generated the humility I expressed in the decision I had to make to return. He took away the anger in my heart and turned my glare towards me. Self-control budded in its place? He broadened my perspective of my mother and gave me the ability to see her not as my mother but as a person. He revealed that I had something invaluable to offer her because she wanted to believe in me. I was permitted to utilize the love I had found as a vehicle to move the obstacles of life before me out of the way so she could see what she desired for me for herself.

The Holy Spirit was always there. In the wee hours of the morning when the devil had me alone, the Holy Spirit would strengthen and encourage me to hold on. He told me not to rely on myself and not to rely on what I hear and feel in my heart. I was told to believe and trust in God and His Word. He reminded me constantly of what was most important in specified situations. My job was to believe and act on my belief in God. When I could not see my way through, He reminded me what is impossible for man is possible with God. He informed me that God could not fail. He told me that God would do all that He said He would do. He provided what I needed in my times of need.

It took faith and submission to the leading of the Spirit when there was no music and no one looking on but God and me. I had to believe God's Spirit was at work after the Sunday experience. As I persisted in my faith the Spirit of God produced the fruit of His presence in my life. My surrender to the control of God produced a sense of peace. God was in control. Things weren't so bad after all. Everything was going to work out. I was changing. It was evident to everyone including myself. It could not be denied. The more I submitted the more I changed. The more I changed the more I knew it was God doing the changing and that everything said in the Word of God was true.

I observed the working of the power of love introduced in me by the Spirit of God. It began to dismantle the walls and other obstructions between my loved ones and myself. I observed the Spirit replace fear with love as the reason for my doing. I saw love establish a willingness in others to try to do better if not to do right. I saw love encourage others to deliver respect and consideration. Everyone didn't take kindness for weakness, just those who are weak themselves.

The Spirit of God opened doors and opportunities in my life. I did not possess the foresight, wisdom or craft to envision of the things that appeared before me. The Spirit of God within me moved beyond me. He closed doors and hearts that were open in my past. He made room behind closed doors that He opened. It was the Spirit of God that empowered me to seize those opportunities within those opened doors.

The Spirit shared freely God's concern for all. He

expressed God's desire to see those called in Christ to be more open to the will of God by faith starting with me. No matter how high a plateau the Spirit of God takes someone, there is room for the flesh to hinder. Sooner or later if we are not careful we will pervert the will of God for our own advantage. That is the nature of man.

All of the greats in the Bible except Jesus were born into sin and had personal sins to atone for: from Cain and Abel to Noah, from Noah to Abraham, from Abraham to David, and from David to us. All have sinned and fallen short of the glory of God. Even your righteousness is as filthy rags. The Spirit of God constantly reminded me of that too. The more God produced in me the more it became necessary to be vigilant. I do not desire to falter in my faith and thwart the plan of God in my life.

The church has reached another plateau in its current history as it relates to the moving of God's Spirit. All around us the world and everything in it is decaying. The world is in denial concerning its state, but the spirit of many is troubled. Church leaders sit at their lofty tables debating one aspect or another of the sin evident everywhere in society paying lip service to the world's reality. The obvious consequences of individual and social wrongs are ignored. America, the last Christian stronghold of the colonial world, is holding on by a spiritual thread because the Church is imbued in the social political mumbo jumbo of the day. We fail to recognize what we see is the work of God's Spirit in the world today.

In ages past the Holy Spirit fell so heavily even the atheistic and the agnostic were swayed to recognize the wisdom and importance of submitting to the people of God. Revivals erupted that led to social awakenings. Traces of those spiritual moves are apparent in every aspect and in every level of society today including the freedom African Americans experience from slavery and blatant oppression in this country.

As the church leaders of New York City gathered as Gatekeepers during the 90's the voice of God clearly spoke and heard. What was said was echoed around the town and throughout the nation. Three points were confirmed by the Spirit and captured the hearts of God's people: remember Christ your first love, the need for ministry to men and prepare for a revival. The Church failed to respond appropriately. If the church continues to refuse to respond to the will of God, He will rise up others and the opportunity to redeem America and therefore impact the world will be lost for this generation.

The key to revival is the unity of the church. To accomplish this it is necessary for the divide within the church to be removed. The divide is constructed of ethnic, racial and class mirages. The divide is spiritual nonsense. There is only one Church Biblically and spiritually. There is only one race, the human race. Clearly differences do exist. We have preferences that distinguish us. If those proclivities must exist in the church they are secondary to the primary realities of the faith.

Galatians 3:26-28 and James 1:9-10 state respectively: for you are all children of God through faith in Christ Jesus. For as many of you as were baptized into Christ have put on Christ. There is neither Jew nor Greek, there is neither slave nor free, there is neither male nor female; for you are all one in Christ Jesus. Let the brother of low degree rejoice in that he is exalted: But the rich, in that he is made low: because as the flower of the grass he shall pass away. The world can and will only know Christ if we who believe love one another. That is the truth concerning the Church and the will of God unto righteousness.

The Holy Spirit is still moving to accomplish the will of God for this church generation. In Deuteronomy the principles governing blessings and curses are explained. The book of Revelation and all it says will come to pass. As much as I desire to see the coming of the Lord I prefer I not be a part of the church generation when the spoken prophecies are fulfilled. If we fail to respond appropriately to the will of God from the plateau He has set us on in the Holy Spirit we leave the doors open for the curses to overtake the Church, the nation and by default the world. If we as a nation housing the national church of Christ in America pick up the mantle placed upon us, there is a good chance God will hear and move on our behalf.

An opportunity was given to the church of New York in the 90's to initiate this work, but the church failed. The men of God retreated to their citadels of faith to hold on to what God had given to them. They forgot the word of God says He who will save his life will lose it, but he who loses his life for my sake shall find it.

Thank God for His mercy and grace. Though the opportunity was missed, there is still time to preserve the nation and prolong God's peace on earth. The Holy Spirit is asking the saints to

380

release Him within the church walls and out into the world on the backs of us who claim to believe. The Holy Spirit is crying in the wilderness beckoning all who can hear to come out of their religious comfort zones within the Church and give birth to a movement of reconciliation.

Some might ask who I am to make such a proclamation. I answer nobody. I ask you who have asked, since you seem to understand the criteria needed to partake in such an endeavor, to come forward in assisting God to accomplish His will. To all others I say we are all nobodies. We are just people who love God. It is God who is calling us according to His will and good pleasure. Do not ignore God's ability and power, which is available to work in you. Look to the hills from which comes our help. You who have born the heat of the sun know that God is more than able to accomplish what He has set out to do in and through you and me. Be encouraged. Do not falter. God is on our side.

## Chapter Eleven

My efforts to attain happiness in life began as a Race struggle that evolved into a class struggle and is concluding as a spiritual struggle. I am arguing the tenants of the Christian faith or debating the benefits of one faith over another. Neither do I want to discuss the realities of existence and its deeper meanings if there are any. What I am addressing is the fact that whatever we are doing, it is not working. There is too much suffering. There is too much hardship and too much is wasted. I believe there are pre-established laws, principles and rules that govern and direct the course of life. These rules need to be leaned, understood and taught religiously to our young and those willing to learn, to reduce the systematic negativity that is pervasive in the African American community and throughout the world at large.

In my pursuit of happiness I see there are no simple solutions. There is no panacea; no one-shot deals and no quick-fix solutions. All success requires hard work and determination. I know I am not the first to make these observations or the first to express a concern. I hope my voice added to the others can make a contribution to the cause of those seeking truth and a better quality of life for all.

Most accept that life begins at our entry onto this earth, on our birthday. We immediately begin to process our environment and if properly cared for we grow and develop. At some point we begin to progressively assume greater and greater responsibility of that process for ourselves. My life was based on learning to survive within that process. What I initially thought to be true was found to be false. What I found to be true at one stage of development I soon realized was false on another. Someone you could trust in one situation you could not trust at another place and time. I learned things could quickly spin out of control and all could be lost if you were not careful. I discovered life was complex on its simplest levels.

To make sense of the madness I set goals and accepted a set of rules to govern my actions. As I grew and recognized discrepancies in my conclusions I revised my rules to maintain some degree of equilibrium. I believed my life was supposed to make sense and it was my job as a human being to discover the sense of it. I currently hold to two precepts that encompass and embody the relevance of my life in all its complexities. The first is the relationship amongst the external, internal and eternal aspects of life. The other is the concept of Accrued Benefits. Both diminished the importance of "self" in my quest to find happiness. With these two precepts and the help of God I hope to be able to influence a turn of events in the lives of others outside of my current sphere of influence.

It became absolutely necessary for me to grasp the relationship amongst what I determined as the external, the internal and the eternal. These aspects of understanding followed a parallel path alongside my human development. I was able to see that in retrospect. The external is roughly defined as everything within the physical realm extending from and including my body outward. It is always tangible. The internal is inclusive of our inner thoughts, beliefs and morals. The internal can be vaguely observed in one's character. It is intangible, but under our control. The eternal is defined as the spiritual. It is both intangible and beyond our control; we can influence it, but mostly we are influenced by it.

Living in and for the external is the lowest level of existence in this triad. Living for and understanding the spiritual is by far superior. All things relate to the spiritual in the end. The internal is directly influenced and directly

384

influences which of the two you live by. Ultimately how you live determines your eternal realities. These factors are not mutually exclusive. They are intricately intertwined with one another and sometimes indistinguishable to the human eye. Due diligence is the only judge.

Accrued benefits relate to advantages and gains applied to a person or group of persons. These gains when attained do not come as a result of one's own efforts or abilities. These privileges are usually assumed by the recipients to be benefits they have earned and have a right to. They are not. They are helps available in life for those who are wise enough to exploit them depending on how you relate to and express the external, internal and eternal.

The factors of these two precepts work together throughout infinite sets and permutations in all aspects of life. My basic understanding of them has allowed me to stay on course in my life.

In my ultimate analysis I have come to know that God is in full control of all things. This is my acknowledgment of the eternal. The trust I have acquired in God has enabled me to take comfort in that fact and find peace within myself. This provides the governance of my internal. The changes that have occurred in my life and the things I have accomplished have proved to me man's dominance over things within life (external), but God has ultimate authority over all things. What He says Goes! Everything within me and around me has improved. The quality of my life, the lives of the members of my family and many others have all been enhanced and enriched because of what I have become.

I have concluded that Jesus Christ is truly the Son of God and Lord of all creation. As a result I have decided to follow Jesus. I believe wholeheartedly He is the answer to all the problems mankind faces in life. There is a song that captures the theme of my spiritual walk. It is titled 'I Have Decided to Follow Jesus'. The chorus says 'No turning back'.

Righteousness is a state God wills all humanity to live within. I applied myself to the level of righteousness God requires. I have a desire to be pleasing in the sight of God. In all my efforts I failed. I found I could not fulfill what I knew God was requiring of me. It was impossible for me to accomplish it in my own strength. I realized if the Word of God was true no human was capable of measuring up to the righteousness of God. The only way it could be done is with God's help. God provided that help in the person of Jesus Christ.

Recognizing that singular fact has made all the difference in my walk with God. Though times were often hard in my walk as my conversion was taking root, there was always the knowledge I was destined to overcome. I knew I was destined because of what God had done and was doing in my life through Jesus Christ.

There is never a dull moment serving Christ. To the untrained eye and the uninitiated it could appear so. Before my initiation I believed serving God was a  waste of time. I believed I was ultimately in control of my own life. It was up to me to make the difference. I determined what I wanted and pursued it. As I encountered obstacles along the way it was my responsibility alone to remove them. All the ups and downs of the pursuit were for my pleasure and excitement. I believed if I reached my goal I would be satisfied. In the end I was disappointed, not satisfied. I was temporarily pleased with my external outcomes, but internally I suffered; I was lowering myself as a person. Spiritually I was dead. I found out it was the life I had chosen that was dull. Life purged me of my ignorance.

Everyone must be purged. You are not righteous. God does not care what you have been told about yourself. Only what He says about you is true.

There are forces that continuously contend with the truths of God and they attack relentlessly to steer you off course. How high you advance spiritually is determined by your willingness to trust, believe and obey God as He directs your life.

The first lines of battle are drawn around yourself. Dr. Maslow calls them needs. We concern ourselves with what we want (external). Sometimes these contentions are not willful. They are instinctive, innate. They are rooted deeply within our being. As you surrender to the knowledge of God and begin to overcome greater understanding is provided. You will begin to develop a degree of effectiveness over other areas of spiritual contention in your life. In Christ there are constant concerns one must address daily. After a while you realize it is the nature of things in this life.

Another area of attack comes from the things present in the world around you. You have to acknowledge that the things of the world are in opposition to God. The things of this world also take issue with the positions you must take to please God. You must develop a Godly worldview (internal). It sounds easy, but it is not.

Lastly there are the dark spiritual forces you must contend with. This is the realm of the devil, his demons and other fallen spirits (eternal). These together are more than enough to keep anyone occupied. If you address God faithfully this will keep you excited and on your toes. Can you do all this alone? No. That is why we need a savior who is available to help us overcome.

To survive through all of this you need a savior. You might have issues with institutional Christianity, you might have problems with individual Christians, but you must not take issue with Jesus Christ and the Word of God. We need Jesus Christ.

In pursuit of my desires obstacles were always and are still presented. My first reaction is to take a good look at myself (internal). I check my motives and my attitudes. If any inconsistencies are found regarding the truths of God I work on making the appropriate personal adjustments with the help of God. If the fault is not found within me a different approach is taken to address the obstacle. If fault is found in me the corrective measures taken are like seeds planted to produce the fruit of my desires in due season. If fault is not found within me a different approach is taken to address the obstacle.

Why do I put myself through all of this? I want the pressures of life lifted off my back. The lighter the burden the easier the journey. I do not want to live hard. I want to see unnecessary problems alleviated. I want to see things improve all around. My greatest burden is for the African American community, the disenfranchised and the under privileged.

The Bible says there is much food in the tillage of the poor, but much is lost because of justice. I want to see more justice. I want to retrieve what's being lost in the tillage of the poor and have God provide for their needs through it. I want to turn the attention of the disadvantaged towards God. I want God to empower and turn the attention of the materially and spiritually disadvantaged towards Him.

The Bible says if you lift up the name of Jesus He would draw all men unto Him. What is the name of Jesus? If you are reading this do you know? We must come to know the name of Jesus. We need to trust more in God. Not in whom you or I say He is, but in whom He says He is. According to God's Word unrighteousness is evident everywhere. It makes its appearance as if it is right. Too many are not given the chance to see righteousness for itself and therefore cannot respond to God's call. People need the opportunity to respond to God's call. I pray ours is the generation God uses to make that call.

It takes courage and strength to respond to the call of God. I pray, no more games. No more enticing words. Put your enemies to shame in the external. Too many deny and mock the reality of God's presence externally. I pray God's eternal presence is manifested in the external world just like He manifested His presence in my life. I pray the Lord God makes a way in this world for His children.

In America we are provided with the constitutional right to freedom of speech. I have the right to say what I believe. The Constitution does not and cannot guarantee the right to speak the truth. Most people believe what they are saying is the truth. I don't believe most of what I see or hear to be the truth. If it is, how come there is so much emotional pain and hatred in life? How come there is no all out attempt to address the root causes of our misery? I am assured that there is a better way. I want to believe in and tell the truth that provides a better way.

God has a purpose and a season for everything under the Sun. A cursory study of God's Word easily reveals God's intentions. Everything written in the Bible will eventually come to pass. The only question is whom will God employ to bring His purposes to pass. Each ethnic group and nation has an assigned purpose. Amidst those peoples are African Americans. There is something that distinguishes the African American. There is something unique about the descendants of those who were brought forcibly to the western hemisphere on slave ships. We are different. Not better, but different. Not worse, different. We are a mighty people. In spite of all we have been through and are still going through in North and South America we have climbed and prospered to the hurt of no one except ourselves. Everything we possess is honestly ours (accrued benefits).

Our distinction goes beyond the color of our skin. Our distinction is found in God's purposes for us as a people. It is our ethos. Our ability to influence and impact other peoples for the good is historically unmatched. The favor we command is phenomenal. We suffer great pain because we are splintered and scattered. It is said despair and apathy has overcome most. There appears to be little hope. Confusion seems to reign in our midst. All appears to be lost. All of this and more is echoed in every corner of our existence except one, the Kingdom of God.

Is there one God? Yes! Is there one Race of Men? Yes! Are all of them equal? Yes! Are all of them the same? No! There are differences and distinctions. Are all Whites the same? No! Are all Blacks the same? No! But we all are equal in the sight of God. Does everybody love God? No. Will everybody love God? No. But that does not mean God does not love them. There is an evil that has invaded the earth.

The Blacks of America have reached a plateau. On the face of things we have assumed heights our forefathers only dreamed of. From our perch we look around and sense we have more coming to us. What we deserve will not come with the assertion of anyone giving us what is due us. What we aspire can only come from our coming together to control our own destiny and demonstrate the power of God in our midst.

With all the apparent foolishness going on in the communities we occupy the problems we face are not our own. These are problems imposed on us by those who have no real love or concern for our well-being. That is the evil we must confront. We must recognize it as evil. We must take a stand against that evil.

That evil is individual. It is systemic It is rational. It is real. Some of us are squirreled away within our personal success stories. In truth you are not. All you have received is an Accrued Benefit. What you have acquired are the benefits of the historical sacrifices made by multiple thousands that made a way for you. God has entrusted His resources into your hands for such a time as this. Do not be afraid. This evil is afraid of us. This evil has always been afraid of us. It has been afraid of our coming together and our unification around any issue. The evil is weakening. Its time is up. It has already been defeated. It is time for us to take another stand in the face of the evil that confronts us. We are the only people who can confront it. It is our fight.

A major asset in our current struggle is the African American male. I took a good look at my situation. My getting right improved the circumstances of all around me. My mother was a good parent. Yet she was not capable of righting the wrong that was in me. I am sure that her prayers for my life are partly responsible for my present condition; it goes without saying the absence of my father created a void that pained her and crippled my family. If my father would

have  stayed I know things would have been
easier.

I know there are many men who are who they are
because of the devotion of their mothers to them.
I commend them and their mothers.
Nevertheless the exception of the rule cannot
negate the rule. For every male who is successful
on the levels suggested I can find two if not more
who are disadvantaged because of the absence of
their fathers. I also need to mention the hurt in
the hearts of my sisters due to the absence of our
father, and the joy that emanated from my
mother when she found I was available as a help
to her as her son,  and also as a man.

Men need to rise up and take greater
responsibility for themselves and their families.
This is often said, but the reality of it scares
everyone. I sometimes wonder why everyone is so
resistant to empowering Black men, including
some Black women. I fear the correct teaching of
Black men is not popular in the world and in the
institutional church because the empowered
Black male is an anathema to current power
structures.

In general when threatened I tend to react
aggressively. In my past I would employ violence.
Aggressive behavior is within my nature. I have

found most men express similar traits. The more challenges I faced the better I became at overcoming threats and challenges with aggression. I learned to stand on my own two feet. I grew in strength and was able to support the weight of others. I became a better man. This world is not interested in better Black men. If there were more of us, the indignities we currently suffer would be eliminated and the world as it is would mourn.

We have too many soft and crippled males in our communities. Too many who are suppressed within the system or controlled by their externals of life. We are in a crisis. There are too many men who have not learned to accept and face life's challenges. We look down upon them and fail to recognize their value. How can we expect a male to become a man if he is not reared to be a man? When was he given that opportunity? We need to look beyond our limited selves to recognize a basic value consistent in masculinity. We must strive to allow opportunities to evolve that permit Black males to become men. Every other people and nation recognizes the value of their men except African Americans and the African American church. Something more must be done.

To be aggressive is not a bad thing. Aggression is an ability like any other. Our men need to learn how to direct their aggressive energies towards constructive measures that benefit someone other than himself alone. The worst thing about us is that we are not collectively constructive. More often than not we concern ourselves with our individual or household self-interests. That is collective self-destruction.

I can no longer tolerate the nonsense everyone is trying to tell me about me (a Black man). Too many Black men are dying and going to jail. This is critical. Most of the images placed before us are negative and superficial. We are psychologically starving to death. Aren't you the best judge of who you are, my brother? Are we not the best judge of whom and what we are? Should someone else's definition of who we are be accepted by us when we disagree with their conclusions? Is this all God has willed for us? Should we accept any definition presented by another that does not contain hope and real solutions for the improvement of our condition?

I am not talking denial here. Are there problems in the Black community? Yes. Are those problems inevitable? I answer with a resounding NNO! We are who God says we are. We are human beings capable of taking charge of our own collective destiny. Anything interfering with, or denying that charge, is not of God and is an enemy of righteousness.

We are spoiled. We have slighted the necessity of putting forth an effort to collectively grow, develop, achieve and prosper. NO PAIN NO GAIN! Men submitted to God are a problem for the devil and a major problem for a sinful world. Men submitted to God can make a major contribution towards the solution to our combined concerns.

Everyone is clamoring about the redevelopment of Harlem. It is evident that many are benefiting from the community's development and I wish them all the best. Personally I do not rejoice with those who herald the new Harlem. I do not believe what is happening in Harlem is in the best interests of African Americans.

I believe we, as African Americans, were sold out by our community leadership and political representatives. There were some who tried. There are several smaller efforts sprouted throughout the community, but not enough to preserve the integrity of the community. The average Harlem resident is being priced out and thereby forced to move out. Too many of the

Black business owners who weathered the difficult years are not in a position to compete with the newer businesses coming in.

If this was standard procedure for every cultural group there could be no complaint. But I see The Chinese benefiting from the development of their neighborhoods. I see Little Italy is still for the Italians. I see the Hasidic Jewish community is still benefiting from activities that occur within their districts. How is it that the most famous Black community in the world, and a symbol of who we are as a people, is be given over to others? Somebody that had the responsibility to consider what was in our best interests betrayed the greater concerns of their constituency for selfish reasons. None of this could have happened in any of the before mentioned ethnic communities.

People have the tendency to see the problems of others while overlooking their own. We think if they were to change their ways everything would be easier. Usually the problem is not outside of us, it is within. It is like a rock thrown into a body of water. Waves in the form of concentric circles emerge to disrupt the serenity of the water. The disruption of the water is not caused by the concentric waves, the disruption of the water was caused by the rock. You are the rock in your water of life. Often the concentric circles of concern you face originate with you. The analogy carries over for the African American as a people.

Every decent mother knows what is in the best interests of their children and household. Anything that comes along and threatens the stability and provision of her family, she resists with all her strength. You cannot fool her. She will not sacrifice any of her children for the supposed benefit of another and she surely would not sacrifice any of her children for the benefit of those outside of her family. Why do we sacrifice ourselves for the betterment of those who are doing fine? It does not make sense unless you are not concerned with the well being of those you are responsible for.

Our collective self-improvement will concentrically impact everything around us for our betterment. What if there is absolute right/good and absolute wrong/bad? What if it is necessary to move towards the supposed absolute right/good and away from what is bad to advance collectively as we did during the Civil Rights Movement? Would it be of value to define what we consider right and good? Wouldn't it also be a worthwhile exercise to apply what we learn and

400

see what good comes out of it? Though the world is going crazy I know there are sane people who want to keep our nation viable for years to come.

I believe there is absolute good and absolute evil. I believe both exist simultaneously. We are the only creatures who can go either way. We can either lean towards good or lean towards evil. We have the ability to stop midstream, turn around and move in the opposite direction. If your bent is towards wrong – stop, turn around, and go the other way. Unlike other creatures of nature we can affect our destiny.

Nobody wants to be called the bad guy. All these bad things are occurring, but in this era of political correctness no one is held responsible except those caught performing the most blatant wrong doings. Somebody other than them is wrong. Something more than that is wrong. In the era of slavery, though no one was ever held accountable for his or her positions, there were a lot of people who supported that vile system and all of them were wrong. A degree of power is essential to perpetuate systemic inequity. It is those with power who make the decisions. It is those with power who establish direction. It is those with power who set the pace. It is those with power who are most responsible.

In the affairs of African Americans we are wrong
for following the crowd. We are wrong because
too many of us have forsaken our heritage and
God given purposes. Let us lay our cards on the
table and see who really cares. Those who do not
care are the enemy of what is good and best.
They have been corrupted and need to be
confronted and addressed. They need to be
addressed like a mother addressing those outside
of her household whose interests threaten the
stability of her home and whose methods
disagree with the rules of justice, equality and
fair play.

Matters that build character are not highly
valued in our community. That is the greatest
deficit of capitalism, which is governed by greed.
(For the record being greedy is bad.) Acquiring
symbols of success accepted by the society at
large is all that matters. Never mind what you do
to acquire them. We have abandoned the
understanding of the profits of having a good
heart. We have been reduced to the level where
individuals possessing such qualities receive
minimal recognition for their contributions. The
larger society pays relative lip service to the
benefits of people with good character.
Encouragement is a wonderful human trait and

support is another. People who exercise good character traits are very useful and significant in any collective. They are the heroes of society.

What is in our collective hearts that allows structured abuses to be continually heaped upon us? What massive fears possess African Americans that we persist in allowing brothers and sisters of our race to be picked off one by one until their outcry becomes an acceptable whimper? Self-interest cannot be the motivating factor African Americans. Self-interest by nature is destructive. No man is an island. We must consider our neighbor and thereby our combined interests. Once determined those interests will be profitable to and universally beneficial to everyone.

The enemies of the many will hold to policies and practices that only apply to the few. Those policies and practices at their core will neglect the well being of all others. God's interest is for the many. I agree with God.

With efforts to elevate conditions in our lives will come the need to elevate the consciousness of our White brothers and sisters. We must let bygones be bygones. Let us redefine the battlefield, the strategy of our conflicts. Let us redefine our enemy. It is not people, but outdated beliefs and practices. The soul of America hangs in the balance. It is the collective soul of our generation that is at stake.

This is the 21 st century. More scientific and technological advances have been made in the previous century than in all the other centuries combined. Let us take advantage of what is known and determine whether humanity is worthy of all this knowledge. Let us determine what is best in it and doggedly strive towards that end.

The legislative supports for racism have been dismantled. America stands before us as the greatest accrued benefit ever amassed and we have not taken full advantage its resources. In no other nation on earth would I have the liberty to pursue my expressed desires. In no other nation on earth could I have come from where I have come from, and have license to move in the direction I am headed. In no other nation on earth could we as a people come from where we have come from, and attained all that we have, but we did. Peoples from every nation strive to get here to improve their station in life. We are here, we always were here and our portion is at hand. Let's do our part to maintain the integrity of America and keep her viable for years to come.

404

Where am I today? I would like to say that I am satisfied, but that would not be the whole truth. On one hand I am totally satisfied and if my life were to end tomorrow I would have no regrets. On the other hand a great sorrow fills my heart because of the confusion, pain and discomforts that persists among those most dear to me. Most of the things that bring on pain and suffering can be avoided. It is usually our ignorance that maintains that condition within our lives. I want to cry out into the wilderness and beckon all to a better way.

Sometimes Christian leaders, in their hearts, position themselves at the top of our faith. That is a grave mistake. I do not condone that error. Christ is at the apex of the faith and He is the epitome of its righteousness. Any and everything less is a failure. I am a failure, but I am thankful for God's grace and mercy as I consider my shortcomings. When more of us are willing to do this we will be able to draw on the promises of God and increase God's holiness within us. That is true power.

People have been telling me what I should or shouldn't do, and what I can or cannot do for most of my life. I have come to find that most have been mistaken. Too many for the most part are misguided, misdirected or misinformed. Not only have I lived free of most restrictions, I have prospered in life. The evolution of one's mind and heart is on a continuum as long as one is open and willing to receive guidance. I believe most of what I have been through is of no consequence in relationship to my pursuit of truth and happiness other than to provide me with a base of knowledge and experience to know what is true. I further argue that the degree of satisfaction I now enjoy could not have been attained unless I had followed the paths I encountered in life.

I find the crux of American culture was to convince me to believe in and desire things that eventually provide no benefit to improving the quality of my life. How well one lives is not just a matter of accumulation of material and monetary resources, a measure of inner peace and health is also essential. Sometimes peace and health is attained without material prosperity. I have observed this fact many times within the African American community. I seek it all for as many who can receive it.

If there is any truth in Christ and any hope for the African American populace, what has been expressed as godliness must be our refuge if we

406

are to truly impact our condition in America and by implication the world.

In the near future I will continue to respond to the call of God in my life and plant a church to preach the unfathomable riches of God to His chosen people. Join me as we take the cause of the Kingdom of God to the next level.

My wife and I leaving church

Top- Out on the town together

Bottom- A man with a heart for children

Top- The girls out with friends       Bottom- Diane Thomas-Wilson

Top- The fruit of faithfulness
Bottom- Love extended beyond bloodlines. The
Hallettes and The Barnwells. The natural
children of Christine Smith.

411

The influence of godliness on the next generation

Getting the message out!

MP3- Men of Promise, Passion and Purpose.

Photo by David Jacobs..

To contact author visit
www.walter.cicoben.com
or write to:
Rev. Walter Wilson
P. O. Box 524292
Bronx, N.Y. 10452

# Christian AutoMotive Services

LOCATED

AT

MUFFLER CITY PLUS

## 1717 WEST FARMS ROAD
## BRONX, NEW YORK
### 10460

WE MINISTER TO ALL YOUR
AUTOMOTIVE NEEDS

PROVIDING QUALITY, INTEGRITY AND
SERVICE

PROFESSIONAL
MECHANICS A WOMAN CAN TRUST

Owners
BROTHER EDWARD OJEDA
REVEREND WALTER WILSON
Call    646-542-3993

TO SCHEDULE YOUR APPOINTMENT TODAY

10% OFF ALL REPAIRS WHEN YOU BRING THIS AD!!!!

---

**THIS IS AN ADVERTISEMENT**

521565